Crisis and Change

The Church in Latin America Today

EDWARD L. CLEARY, O.P.

ORBIS BOOKS

Maryknoll, New York 10545

The Catholic Foreign Mission Society of America (Maryknoll) recruits and trains people for overseas missionary service. Through Orbis Books Maryknoll aims to foster the international dialogue that is essential to mission. The books published, however, reflect the opinions of their authors and are not meant to represent the official position of the society.

Manuscript Editor: William E. Jerman

Library of Congress Cataloging in Publication Data

Cleary, Edward L.
  Crisis and change.

  Bibliography: p.
  Includes index.
  1. Catholic Church—Latin America.   2. Latin
America—Church history.   I. Title.
BX1426.2.C54   1985   282.8   84-16478
ISBN 0-88344-149-7 (pbk.)

Contents

Preface

A few years ago a U.S. Army general who had been active in Latin American affairs and then dropped out to devote his time to other parts of the world was reassigned to duty that would take him to Latin America. The Pentagon thought it was a good idea to bring the general up to date, so a one-hour briefing session was arranged for him.

The colonel who did the briefing, an academic person, was aware of the absurdity of trying to bring someone up to date on twenty-two countries over a ten-year period. Nonetheless, both men went ahead. The general bore manfully the onslaught of disparate events and conflicting tendencies. He never took a note but his attention never wavered.

At the end, the colonel took a deep breath and asked the general if he had any questions or observations. "No," he said. "No questions. It's the same old story: the leftists trying to start something, the military stepping in, and the church running between the both of them trying to conciliate."

But it is not always the same old story. The following pages document why one cannot presume Latin America remains unchanged. For one thing, essential changes have taken place in political factors in Latin America, and the social and political situation in the region will never be the same again.

This book has been twenty-two years in the making. It results from living in Latin America for a number of years and of revisiting there many times, often as editor of a social science journal dealing with Latin America. When the writing was being done, many experiences of those years were relived, so that joys of friendship special to Latin America, pleasures of an expressive culture, and the frustrations and hopes of many Latin American friends came vividly to mind.

But personal experiences had to be overshadowed by the larger drama taking place in Latin America. One cannot study, interview, interpret, and reconstruct the contemporary history of Latin America and its institutions without feeling joy at changes and growth, sorrow over death or disappearance, frustration over fated collisions. The sensitive reader, too, will experience many of these joys, sorrows, and frustrations.

One cannot read of events of recent years in Latin America without sharing in the lives of the characters in the drama. Nor are the persons involved in Latin American conflicts faceless symbols of a struggle of good and evil; moreover, they often share many basic values. Generals Hugo Banzer of Bolivia and Augusto Pinochet of Chile are men of deep Christian convictions. During the writing of this work they became as real to me as my grandparents. Archbishop Oscar Romero of El Salvador and Father Luis Espinal of Bolivia were men of profound Christian commitment. They were known through personal contacts over the years. Both were murdered, probably at the order of or with the toleration of the military.

As a result of sharing in the drama, one may wish to do something about the situation, by way of passing on to others knowledge of the situation, of helping to change U.S. foreign policy, or even of living more simply. But the only direct intention I had in mind was recounting what is taking place in Latin America and in the Catholic Church as accurately as possible. The story is so powerful and dramatic that it needs no embellishment of imagination or rhetoric.

The main elements of the contemporary situation are social and political. It is a drama of social conflict, social movement, and large-scale institutions. It is also a story of networks and ideology. Hence, the chief tools of description and interpretation are those of social science, especially anthropology and sociology.

The groups to which this work is primarily directed are students in social sciences, religious studies, and Latin American studies.

Debts of gratitude for assistance in the completion of the work are extensive due to the travels of two years that took me to Miami, Pittsburgh, New York, and Latin America. I am deeply grateful to the Dominican Province of St. Albert (U.S.A.) for grants received, and to the communities at Pleasantville and New York for fraternal support.

The book was written while I was a research associate at the Columbia University Institute of Latin American and Iberian Studies and at the Research Institute for the Study of Man. I express profound gratitude to Vera Rubin of the Research Institute for the Study of Man and Lambros Comitas of Columbia University, Mark Rosenberg of Florida International University, and also to Carmelo Mesa-Lago of the University of Pittsburgh. As directors of institutes or centers, each offered environments that facilitated the completion of a complex task. They and their staffs offered warm reception, generosity, and encouragement.

A number of colleagues at those institutions helped in the formulations of ideas expressed herein; they cannot be blamed for inadequacies that may exist. Construction of the work was aided by discussions with those mentioned above and with James Malloy, Cole Blasier, José Moreno, Anthony Maingot, Harold Sims, John Risley, and Lawrence and Mary Hall. Thomas O'Meara helped substantially in planning the book. Thomas Quigley of the U. S. Catholic Conference and William Wipfler of the National Council of Churches assisted at various times.

1

A New Leadership:
From Inertia to Momentum

No one could have predicted the changes that were to take place in the Roman Catholic Church in the 1960s. They were extensive and dramatic. But they did not come into being without preparatory steps.[1] The inevitability of change and the outline of the overall picture could be perceived only after all the parts had come together.

There are no leaps in history without something to leap from. This chapter and the book that follows trace an unusual course of social evolution, in that few saw the changes coming. I want to begin by looking at the more important precedents of change in the Latin American church.

Even longtime observers of the Latin American scene did not realize that apparently unrelated events or movements in the 1950s and early 1960s would converge and bring about immense consequences. How did outsiders and insiders alike miss the large-scale changes that were about to take place? How could academics and ambassadors take for granted that the Latin American church would remain an unchanging, fiesta-bound, otherworldly monolith? Neither theologians nor church leaders expected profound and comprehensive changes in Latin American Catholicism.

1

The Roman Catholic Church was part of the status quo in Latin America. Observers formed stereotypical images of the church in Latin America. To begin to comprehend what has taken place in that institution one first has to realize that the church in Latin America is in crisis. Many Protestants, however, think that Roman Catholicism and Latin America, from 1900 to 1965, remained unchanged:

> To most Protestants these [changes] were strange and uncomfortable phenomena. Anti-Catholic polemic had been a familiar stance. We had become accustomed to applying the analytical scalpel and baring the error, corruption, and heresy of the Roman Church. We were skilled at attributing to Roman Catholic dogma all the ills of Latin American culture and society. Even our own doctrine tended to be defined in antithesis. Conversion was often conceived of in terms of leaving the superstition of Rome for the enlightenment of the evangelical church.[2]

Protestant theologian José Míguez Bonino spoke of "tensions of a Catholicism pulled in one direction by its ancient alliances with centers of power, in another by its concern to be in touch with people."[3] W. Dayton Roberts, an Evangelical missionary in Latin America, added: "The current effort of Romanism to identify with the poor and underprivileged, after centuries of being part and parcel of the ruling hegemony, is consequently a tearing, painful process."[4]

The rates of change within the church varied widely from country to country. The progressive leadership of the Brazilian and Chilean churches advanced these churches through changes in the 1950s and early 1960s, while portions of the Mexican and Central American churches adopted new approaches in the 1970s. The majority of Latin American Catholics remained unchanged in the first two-thirds of this century, bound by inertia. Moreover, a minority of traditional Catholics in Latin America and in the Vatican opposed proposals for changes in ideology or practices that appeared in Latin America. Against that background significant persons or groups described below played active leadership roles in changing the ideology and practices of Latin American church.

I turn now to six factors or movements that led to gradual modernization of the Latin American church between 1900 and 1965: lay movements, influx of foreign religious personnel, formation of transnational and national structures, papal nuncios, new ecclesial leadership groups, and John XXIII and Vatican II.

Signs of Life: Lay Movements

A major sign of new life in the Latin American church was the formation and growth of a number of lay movements. They began appearing in the first two decades of this century as organizations of militant lay persons with close ties to their local priests and bishops. They derived their inspiration from Leo XIII's *Rerum Novarum* (1891). The movements served several purposes: defense of Catholic interests against secularistic or anti-Catholic governments, promotion of social justice (better working conditions, just wages), and promotion of "Catholic culture" (public expression of faith through outdoor ceremonies and pilgrimages, dedication of the nation to God, instruction in Catholic teaching in public schools). Some movements of this era focused on workers or farmers but the most notable utilized well-educated or well-placed lay persons in attempts to influence national policy or to defend the place of the church in society. Typically the movements had no ties with other Latin American groups or with lay movements in Europe.

These early movements seldom remained effective for more than a few years of often intense activity. For the most part, they lacked bureaucratic structures for recruitment, selection, and training that would have aided survival and growth. Instead the movements depended almost wholly upon the charisms of a single individual, usually a priest or bishop, and resulted in a personalistic following that continued for the relatively short life of an ad hoc cause.

Catholic Action

The most important lay movements began after 1930. Chief among them was *Acción Católica*, Catholic Action.[5] It was to become a major factor in the life of the Latin American church, though it is seldom mentioned in general Latin American histories. Catholic Action emphasized a distinct and active role for lay persons, an innovation of some consequence in a culture where lay persons were expected to be faithful, passive members of the church. Catholic Action was this-worldly. It demanded activity, not *discusiones a café*. It had international ties, especially to Europe. It nurtured a whole generation of leaders, many of whom rose to positions of national political or intellectual leadership.

At first, in the 1930s, Latin American Catholic Action tended to follow the Italian model of Catholic Action, generalized, embracing all social categories of Catholics. Later, especially after 1945, it tended to follow specialized models of French and Belgian derivation, based on the work of Canon (later Cardinal) Joseph Cardijn. This later model developed three largely autonomous branches to recruit young men and women who were farmers, workers, or students. The goal of Catholic Action was for lay persons to influence the secular milieu in which they worked. In small cells or groups they were to *see* and describe the situation in which they worked or lived, to *judge* the situation in the light of Christian principles (such as justice and charity), and then to *act* realistically to correct or enhance their milieu.

It is worth noting that this model of Catholic Action is sometimes thought to imitate communist organization and tactics. It was no accident that the organizational structure of the French model of Catholic Action resembled the interlocking cells of the Communist Party. But the methodology of see-judge-act (even if it owed something to Marxist praxis) came from Thomas Aquinas's teaching on prudence.

The three Latin American branches of the French model, JAC (Juventud Agrícola Católica), JOC (Juventud Obrera Católica), and JUC (Juventud Universitaria Católica) grew at differing rates. Thousands joined JAC in Argentina, but it was virtually unknown in neighboring Bolivia. Brazilian JOC increased from 15,000 members in 1953 to 120,000 in the mid-1960s. But in other countries Catholics often opted for Catholic Action in the larger sense and created labor leadership schools (as in Bolivia) or Catholic labor unions (such as CLASC, which operated in Venezuela and other countries), instead of joining JOC.[6]

In most Latin American countries where specialized Catholic Action was growing the favored branch was JUC. Its major goal was control of national student movements and of secular universities through student participation in their *co-gobierno* (a privilege won in Córdoba in 1918 and thereafter extended to many other Latin American universities). JUC won many local and national student elections; the cause it opposed in the 1950s and early 1960s was communism.

Catholic Action, appearing as early as 1920 in Cuba, 1930 in Argentina, 1935 in Costa Rica and Peru, and 1938 in Bolivia, gained significant size and influence in the 1950s and '60s. By 1953 the time was ripe for an important climax: the II Interamerican Study Week at Chimbote, Peru.[7]

The meeting foreshadowed decisive changes in the Latin American church. Some observers, such as Helmut Vitalis, have seen the event as the turning point in Latin American Catholicism.[8] Delegates from twenty Latin American countries gathered for the meeting. They began with a lengthy, if somewhat clumsy, description of the Latin American church. They agreed that most Latin American Catholics were only nominally Catholic, with only an appalling minimum of religious instruction. They could be expected to reflect but nominal acceptance of the spirit and dictates of the gospel. Their Catholicism consisted of a traditional set of pious customs, a superficial substitute for those demands of a vital nature that the gospel made upon their lives. Latin American Catholicism needed a profound revitalization.

The Chimbote delegates attempted to describe the socioeconomic, cultural, and political context of Latin American Catholicism. Their description is not so interesting for its content as for its description of social and political realities—a major part of the final document, giving it a this-worldly character that was not typical of Latin American Catholicism. The constructive and objective approach that the Chimbote delegates took continued in their discussion of the Protestant presence in Latin America. They urged civil tolerance and freedom of worship. They urged love, rather than hostility, for Protestants.

The Chimbote report remained a guide for Catholic Actionists for the next few years. The IV Interamerican Catholic Action Week reaffirmed three years later the Chimbote conclusions. Moreover, the report was referred to the first Lay Apostolate Congress in Rome in 1957. Events and consciousness anticipated a new era. A giant was beginning to awake.

Although the social positions of Catholic Action members were

open and advanced, their political positions in 1953 were generally conservative. Little by little Catholic Action was entering a
crisis, a crisis caused not so much by an opening to Marxism or
socialism but by something more fundamental: the rationale behind Catholic Action had to be changed.

Gustavo Gutiérrez describes the dilemma well: he himself suffered through it as national adviser to the Catholic Student Movement in Peru.[9] Gutiérrez saw a church at the service of the world.
Further, there were not two histories, two worlds—religious and
secular; there was only history. This represented an enormous
shift in thinking. Previously, in the 1950s and early 1960s, Catholic Actionists attempted to set up a "New Christendom" in Latin
America. They had promoted political parties, labor unions, student organizations, and newspapers "of Christian inspiration."
Throughout Latin America appeared parties such as *Ação Popular* and Christian Democracy, unions such as CLASC, newspapers such as *Presencia* (the largest daily newspaper in Bolivia),
and university student parties, to serve as the political arm of
Catholic Action.

The Cursillo Movement

In the late 1950s, especially after the massive influx of missionaries from Europe and North America, a number of other major
lay movements developed. These included the Christian Life
Community (popularly known as the Jesuit Sodality before
1968), the Legion of Mary, the St. Vincent de Paul Society, and
the Union of Christian Employers and Managers. Some of these,
such as the Christian Family Movement, were to achieve considerable influence in the Andean region and the Caribbean. Particularly important were the *Cursillos de cristiandad* (Short Courses
in Christianity) in which millions of Latin Americans participated. In Santo Domingo, capital of the Dominican Republic, some
50,000 persons have made a Cursillo.

One "makes" a Cursillo: they are such intense experiences that
they are recalled in terms of creativity. Spanish Bishop Juan Hervas with Eduardo Bonnín and other Spanish laymen introduced
in 1949 and refined over a few years the content and techniques of
the Cursillo. Exportation from Spain to Latin America began in

the late 1950s and the movement spread quickly but unevenly to one then another Latin American country. The movement peaked in the early 1960s and diminished severely after Vatican Council II in the Andean countries. Nonetheless the Cursillos continue strong in some Central American and Caribbean countries.

To counteract the preference of many Latin American men to leave the practice of religion to women, Spanish founders of the Cursillo and Latin American directors limited enrollment to men. Curious and not wishing to be excluded from something that had affected husbands or fiancés, Spanish and Latin American women petitioned for some years to participate in the Cursillos. Their request was granted but the general policy continued that when the Cursillo movement began in a new place only men were invited for the first year or two.

Prospective *cursillistas* often were screened before being invited to participate and the invitation was often considered to be a call to membership in an elite. Certain types were excluded: persons whose marriage could not be recognized by the church, those described as "loosely packaged," and those thought dominated by their spouse. Preference was given to leadership types, persons known to be able to influence others, and those who held important positions in government or business.

Typically thirty to forty men or women make a Cursillo; thirteen lay persons and a priest direct it. A lay person, called the rector, acts as overall director; the priest acts as spiritual advisor; the other twelve lay persons are called professors (in fact, they act as co-directors and often as spiritual advisors and animators). All are carefully schooled in the Cursillo method.

Although the Cursillo often appears as a spontaneous experience, even the jokes, laughter, and music are scheduled. Hervas and his followers permit little deviation in the structuring of the Cursillo. The three-day experience starts with an overnight retreat, beginning on a Thursday evening and continuing to midday Friday. The *cursillistas* maintain silence and the directors foster an atmosphere of reflection. For many participants the retreat period offers the opportunity to "shift gears" from a hectic life, to perceive that something important is going to take place, and to dwell on obstacles that kept them back from full participation in Christian life.

After noon on Friday the fifteen spiritual talks begin, followed by intense and frank discussion that form the core of the Cursillo experience. Lay professors give ten of the talks and the priest gives the remaining five. The talks sum up the essence of Christianity, following traditional church concepts with some modification for recent theological formulations. The professors speak from personal experience (sometimes to the point of revealing their own dramatic failures) and relate the substance of their talk to the life of the laity—problems that men and women face in the world today. Therein lies much of the impact of the Cursillo: profound and intense presentation, and endorsement by respected community leaders.

The Cursillo has a strong impact on most participants. Sudden and "surprise" conversions of "public sinners" or high officials (sometimes the two are the same) are well known. Many lay men and women participating actively in the church or in the role of the church in society owe their commitment to the Cursillo experience.

Nonetheless criticisms of the movement are numerous. Many *cursillistas* drift off to remain uncommitted. (Cursillo originators attempted to forestall slippage by means of a "Fourth Day," a continuation of the Cursillo experience through weekly or monthly follow-up meetings called *Ultreya* ["beyond"].) Some dismiss the Cursillo as a pre-Vatican II movement that prepares lay persons for duty in a clerical church. Whatever its failings, the Cursillo exposed millions, even if fleetingly, to a vision of the essence of Christianity, something many had not seen before.

In sociological terms, the lay movements represented the church's effort to capture the loyalties of and to mobilize key status groups—farm workers, urban workers, intellectuals, and students. These groups were often the target of Protestant missionaries or of the secular left. The church needed new structures to do this and it created lay movements as part of organizational specialization in local church systems. Changes in the structures of the church and in the work carried on within those structures become more evident in the consideration of two major happenings in the Latin American church prior to the Medellín Conference: the massive influx of religious personnel from North America and Europe, and the formation of the Latin American Episcopal Council (CELAM).

Missionary Influx

A phenomenon that illustrates well the changing nature of the Catholic Church as a transnational agency is the sending and receiving of thousands of clerical and lay missionaries to Latin America in the 1950s and '60s.[10] Missionaries of diverse nationalities have been going to Latin America since colonial times but, after the first wave of Spaniards, missionaries tended to arrive sporadically and in small numbers. The first, large, modern influx began during World War II due to the blocking of mission areas, especially in the Far East. The second modern influx, larger in extent, began in the mid-1950s and reached its climax in the mid-1960s.

In large part the missionaries came because of a dearth of native clergy. The expulsion of Spanish priests from most Latin American countries in the nineteenth century and the hardships and limitations imposed on the church by newly formed republican governments caused a precipitous decline in the number of priests and religious brothers, a decline from which the Latin American church has never fully recovered. Before the wars of independence in the 1800s, there was one priest or brother for about every 1,000 persons; by 1890 there was one priest or brother for every 3,000 persons; and by 1930 and thereafter, one for every 5,000 persons. Pastoral care on all but a selective basis becomes virtually impossible under such conditions.

Among the first to call attention in the U.S.A. to the situation were the Maryknoll missionaries, who turned their energies to Peru, Bolivia, and Chile instead of China and Japan during World War II. Foremost among them was John Considine, who argued for a massive sending of religious personnel, clerical and lay, for Latin America."[11] Pope John XXIII (1958–63) exerted special efforts to interest and motivate religious orders and diocesan priests from the United States and Canada to go to Latin America. This was symbolized concretely by a papal request in 1961 that religious orders send 10 percent of their members to Latin America. That voluntary quota was never fully realized, but thousands of priests, brothers, and sisters went from North Atlantic bases to work in Latin America. They were joined by lay men and women who served through PAVLA

(Papal Volunteers for Latin America) and similar organizations.

The implications of that influx have not been fully explored (or even alluded to by many leading Latin American historians). It meant the importation of new ideas and lifestyles. It also meant new cultural motivations and expectations. For the receiving church, there was a reverse cultural shock. One has only to imagine what it would mean to a relatively small national church, as in Bolivia, to receive in ten years a 60 percent increase in religious personnel. The Bolivian church received personnel from the U.S.A., Canada, Spain, Italy, Germany, France, Holland, Belgium, and Ireland—to name only the most numerous national groupings. The Latin American church could never be the same again. Moreover, through these foreign personnel, advances of the Latin American church were quickly and often approvingly communicated to churches of the developed world.

The isolation of the churches of the Americas began to disappear. The U.S. and Canadian churches, as young churches, had earlier concentrated their efforts on working with hordes of immigrants. With declining immigration and with large numbers of religious personnel after World War II, the U.S.A. and Canada were in a position for the first time to turn their interests to the church beyond their borders. As Archbishop Joseph Bernardin, former executive secretary of the National Council of Catholic Bishops, remarked: "Before 1960 there were not ten bishops in the United States who knew the names of five bishops in Latin America."[12] Participation in joint missionary effort was to change that.

Creation of CELAM and National Councils

Another major event in the transnational character of the Latin American church was the formation in 1955 of CELAM, the Latin American Episcopal Council. CELAM holds ordinary conferences every year and extraordinary conferences about every ten years. The first extraordinary conference, at Rio de Janeiro in 1955, is forgettable; the second, at Medellín, Colombia, in 1968, and the third, at Puebla, Mexico, in 1979, are not. The conference in Rio, although having little memorable to say, is recalled for being the first time the church came together in Latin America and for creating CELAM as a permanent transnational entity.

Efforts at establishing a Latin American church council had long been afoot. The first meeting of the Latin American bishops took place at Rome in 1899. It was too early for the formation of a regional body. In a continent where letters took two months to arrive at their destination, if arrive they did, the likelihood of effective communication needed as a basis for international interaction was lacking.

North Americans do not realize how organizationally weak the Latin American church has been. In contrast to the long-standing National Council of Bishops and Canadian Bishops Council, Latin American organizational activity and structuring at national and regional levels are of recent origin. For an institution that is transnational by its very nature, the expansion of international linkages, structures, and activity in the Latin American church are major developments.

The implications for those who cooperate or compete with the Roman Catholic Church are enormous. The consequences for international communism, Protestant church bodies, the U.S. State Department, the Latin American military establishment, and Latin American governments are only partly understood by them. President Carter in 1979 ordered U.S. intelligence to monitor closely the phenomenon of the Latin American church and especially its more active elements.

As the 1950s began, the Latin American church was structurally weak at the national and international levels for two reasons: the basic structural nature of the church and the lack of development of infrastructures throughout much of its territory. From its foundation the Catholic Church has been structured basically into dioceses. These "local churches" are geographical units centered around a bishop. In some mission territories prelatures are governed by administrators given various titles; they too are geographical units—on their way to becoming dioceses. In effect the globe is divided into units administered by a bishop or the equivalent. These administrators relate directly to Rome. There is a sense in which there is no place in primitive Christian theology or practice for national or regional bodies. Nonetheless there are compelling reasons for organizational coordination and activity at those levels.

Secondly, Latin America has been characterized by weakness of infrastructures: highways, airlines, telephone systems, intermediate governing structures, and the like. Thus, it is no surprise at all in a country where there are only two paved highways that one bishop has very little idea of what another bishop is doing or planning.

Only as airline communication reached a more extensive level did the possibilities of national and regional councils open up. (A train ride from La Paz to Buenos Aires [approx. 1,400 miles as the crow flies] could take five days.) National church councils in general are still organizationally weak in resources. Nevertheless, their creation has meant a qualitative difference in the organizational capacity of the church. Inasmuch as most social or religious issues have a national character, national councils enable the church to address them in a more comprehensive and effective fashion. Then too, the national conferences give the bishops more influence. It is one thing for the president of Bolivia to deny the request of Jorge Manrique, archbishop of La Paz, that a foreign priest not be expelled; it is quite another thing for the president to face the "demand" of the national council of bishops to keep hands off. In addition, the national conferences have been able to identify and disseminate theological or pastoral innovations through national offices of education or pastoral planning. With the formation of national conferences and their specialized departments, the rapid dissemination of new ideas became possible. A relatively remote place such as La Paz learned quickly what was going on at Ivan Illich's Center for Intercultural Formation in Cuernavaca, Mexico, or what further ideas Paulo Freire in Chile (in the early 1970s) had about adult education. The National Office of Catholic Education acted as a listening post for those progressive ideas. From the La Paz office, these ideas spread through newsletters and informal channels to dioceses and parishes.

The same organizational gains have been made at the regional level through CELAM. Talented, well-trained staff members were recruited from many Latin American countries for CELAM departments, such as education, CELAM institutes, such as catechetics at Medellín, and CLAR, the Latin American Conference of Religious (men and women who belong to religious orders or congregations). CELAM publication of documents, studies, and popular treatments of updated theology or worship has been elaborate.

Although CELAM itself is now housed in a large headquarters in Bogotá, the building itself is a symbol of outside dependence by the Latin American Episcopal Council. It took twelve years to be realized: the Latin American church is relatively weak in terms of finances. It depends heavily for support on outside sources, especially West Germany and the United States, a factor that hampers full independence of the Latin American church.

Vatican Envoys: Formal and Informal Roles

Few analyses of the Latin American church take into account the structured transnational character of the Roman Catholic Church, precisely in the person and role of the nuncios in each country. Three sets of formal ties link the Latin American church to the central church organization in Rome. First, individual bishops are interrelated with the pope directly or indirectly through the Roman Curia, the upper level of the Vatican organizational structure. Secondly, CELAM has strong ties with Rome through the Pontifical Commission for Latin America. Thirdly, papal nuncios represent the Vatican in individual countries and in turn are tied to the Vatican through the Secretariate of State. Both CELAM and the nuncios furnish the church with formal organizational linkages across national lines.

Some nuncios have also been important figures in atypical ways. Historians or social scientists mention on occasion Archbishop Cesare Zacchi in Cuba or Archbishop Emmanuele Clarizio in the Dominican Republic. However, from a social science perspective, episodic events are insufficient. One must also uncover and analyze formal and informal structures within organizations, structures that in this case furnish transnational linkages.

The roles nuncios have played in the Latin American church go beyond their official delineation. Vallier defines nuncios in terms of their role specialization: diplomacy. He sees their specialization as built around a relational system. "Within this system nuncios are oriented to officials in sovereign states. . . . Relations between the Holy See and sovereign states are critical for regular religious work in the field. Without the proper 'working condi-tions' at the national level, the church cannot proselytize and can-not make contact with residential bishops, and through them, with the faithful."[13] In Vallier's view the role of the nuncio is the securement of conditions favorable to activity in political sys-tems. The nuncio thus becomes a critical agent in the transna-tional system of the Latin American church. Further, the role definition of the nuncio is both similar to and fuller than that of an ambassador.

The nuncio performs other formal and informal roles that Val-lier and others overlook. A particularly important formal role is their part in the selection of bishops. Nuncios review, character-ize, and recommend those who have been postulated as candi-dates for the episcopacy by the grass roots or by other bishops. Nuncios have also been important informal political figures in national as well as ecclesiastical affairs. From the point of view of bishops, nuncios are not supposed to interfere in the internal af-fairs of the local church. But nuncios do act in internal affairs.

For their part, nuncios lament that such interventions were or are necessary. "There was no one else," or "The church here was so weak, I had to step in," Nuncio Rómulo Carboni was accus-tomed to say about his activities in Peru. What he meant was that until recently there was no formal structure of consequence at the national level or that local bishops did not know how to interact nationally for joint political strategy or how to represent their interests in international circles.

Nuncios have attempted to influence repressive governments and motivate them to improve the human rights situation. In such instances nuncios may end up defending the rights of activist priests or lay persons with whose ideology they may disagree. Nuncios have been influential in forging certain political compro-mises, as in Cuba and the Dominican Republic. Papal representa-tives have also been very important in Latin America for the obtaining and channeling of resources (money and personnel) from other national churches, especially those of the North Atlantic.

The nuncio as entrepreneur was best illustrated by Archbishop Rómulo Carboni, for ten years papal nuncio in Peru. After he arrived in Peru, in 1959, Carboni traveled tirelessly all over the country. He visited more places than even peripatetic President Fernando Belaunde in his first presidency. Carboni worked up a plan for Peru. He asked all the bishops for essential data about their diocese. A compilation was translated into English, printed, and sent to all the bishops and religious superiors of Canada and the United States. The result was phenomenal. One hundred fifty religious communities from other countries sent personnel to Peru. Of all U.S. diocesan priests who went to Latin America, 68 percent went to Peru. Carboni also acted in the coordination needed between sending and receiving churches.

The informal roles played by nuncios have far exceeded their formal role definition. Their wider activities, even when believed to be necessary, were also annoying in the eyes of local church authorities who resented the intrusion of outsiders in their internal affairs. (Eventually Carboni had to leave Peru because of his repeated interference.) The nuncios' wider role definition had been a response to a power vacuum; with the creation and strengthening of national church councils, nuncios have tended to retreat to narrower and stricter role definitions. Nonetheless, they are important linkages for the church as a transnational body.

Informal Networks and New Leadership Groups

Surrounding the conferences formed at the national and regional levels are informal networks of intellectuals and activists. Their number is difficult to determine with accuracy but the relative size and shape can be gauged from events such as the Puebla conference (1979) and through formal network analysis done some years earlier.[14] There is more than a single network of religious thinkers; the networks of intellectuals, planners, and activists tend to intersect and overlap. These networks are the driving force of the Latin American church. At the core is a group of intellectuals, most of them active in the elaboration of theology of liberation. This group, at least at the Puebla conference, numbered about thirty persons. This is almost exactly the same group that came together for the major meeting of Latin American theologians in 1975 at Mexico City

Theologians act as the inner force of the Latin American church, and another network functions as the connecting force.

This group is worldwide but its tightest connections are between the Latin American countries and the triangle of North America, South America, and Western Europe. These groups came to know one another through CICOP (Catholic Inter-American Cooperation Program) meetings in the U.S.A. (1964–71), Vatican Council II (1962–65), World Council of Churches meetings at various times, and through Third World ecumenical meetings, such as that held in Dar es Salaam (1976).[15] Participants in the core connecting network are international and ecumenical in outlook. They are well educated, well traveled, and urgent about what they are doing.

One should look beyond the networks themselves to focus on individual members, for they represent new churchmen, new religious types. Anthropological and sociological researchers working in largely primitive and peasant cultures identified distinct types of religious leaders: shaman, magician, and priest. Max Weber favored the magician-priest-prophet trinomial. Research in complex cultures has added mystic, founder, reformer, and saint. A more contemporary description will be suggested here.

The new religious figures comprise a group of articulate and active Christian advocates and strategists. This group has emerged globally during the last three decades, and in Latin America during the last two decades. The boundaries of the group are far from distinct. But there is little doubt about the broad criteria defining membership.

To be a member of the new front-line group one must be—typically—an ordained priest or minister, or even a bishop, although some of the newer members, such as Enrique Dussel and Rosemary Ruether, are lay persons. The fact of ordination gives a stamp of authenticity to someone's descriptions or evaluations of an inside situation. A new member has also—typically—been associated with some dramatic public event, such as publishing a controversial book, setting forth some sort of program, or being involved in an ecclesiastical crisis or major event such as the Puebla or Medellín conferences. This provides him (typically male) with visibility and a reputation. Observers can take positions for or against him and gain a sense of participation through evaluation of his reputation and activities.

The new ecclesial pathbreakers have little in common with confessionally oriented believers. Their field is the whole Christian enterprise—and beyond that, the universe. They do not attempt to promote Roman Catholicism, Lutheranism, or Methodism. Instead they focus on the universal church and the modern world. In most cases, they are cosmopolitan, deeply involved in the urban world (often in direct contact with the poor) and in international activities. Their common milieu provides them with a basis for international rapport and makes possible the continual exchange of ideas through formal media, if not through interpersonal contact.

As implied, the new leaders are sociologically oriented: they use either sociological concepts and research findings or sociological metaphors in their theological reasoning. Such topics as doctrine, belief, worship, and evangelization are dealt with frequently in relation to sociological principles concerning status, group behavior, institutions, influence, and conflict. Typically, though, they are weak in formal political analysis, and such key concepts as power and policy-making are not well dealt with.

The new leaders tend to be engaged in two or more diverse types of professional activity. They may combine pastoral work with missionary concerns, professional duties in a school of theology or university with secondary pastoral duties, planning and research activities in special areas such as ecumenism with an interest in the training and professional problems of the clergy, or journalistic work with chaplaincy duties. Latin American participants in the new networks are, above all, involved with and driven by concern for the poor and the oppressed.

Many of the new leaders hold memberships on or serve as consultants to high-level church (and sometimes government) committees. They are involved with international agencies of coordination and implementation, such as institutes sponsored by CELAM, most of the important internal groupings in CELAM itself (until recently), commissions carrying on the work of Vatican II, key departments of the World and National Council of Churches (Geneva and New York), and the Confederation of Evangelical Churches in Latin America. However, all their involvement with the ecclesiastical establishment is characterized by the maintenance of the critical, open posture that is a trademark of the new ecclesial leadership.

John XXIII and Vatican II

The sixth factor that changed the Latin American church happened outside Latin America: the election of John XXIII and the call for Vatican Council II. John with his warmth, effusiveness, and openness to religions and cultures outside Europe set in motion the aggiornamento, the updating of the Catholic Church, that was soon to touch the Latin American church in a variety of ways. The most significant impulse for change was the four-year experience of Vatican II. But many other initiatives for change in Latin America were taken during the five-year reign of Pope John. One of the most influential of these was the Ten-Year Plan of Aid to Latin America, which included the call for 10 percent of religious personnel to be sent there from Europe, Canada, and the United States. John, by force of his personality and vision, created an atmosphere of hope, creativity, and outreach.

The most important event in the life of the Latin American church in almost five hundred years of existence was the experience of Vatican Council II. The council brought Latin Americans into daily contact with church leaders from all over the world and it forced submerged issues to the surface. Moreover, it set in motion or reinforced a whole series of properly Latin American initiatives that are the subject of the remainder of this book: Latin American theology, grassroots movements, new authority relationships, and critical stands on social issues.

The announcement of the Second Vatican Council was heard like a cannon shot across most of Latin America. The initiative coming from Rome had been as unexpected as the election of John XXIII. Dutifully but still in mild shock, Latin American bishops and their advisors prepared for the council. It would be the first time in history that Latin American bishops would participate in a church council in numbers proportionate to the Latin American percentage of the world Catholic population.

The very fact of their profusion would make the Latin American church conspicuous: it was the largest in the world. Over 600 bishops and 319 *periti* from Latin America participated in the council. But whether the Latin American church would be up to playing a major role was another story.

Almost a year was spent in preparation for the council. The Latin American church found itself scurrying. Consultations were held with active lay groups, with practically anyone who could be called a theologian, and with *periti* (that loosely defined group of experts who would advise bishops). Many of these advisors accompanied their bishops to Rome and some participated directly in the council. But except for having a part to play in the preparation of one document and the occasional noteworthy interventions of a few Latin American bishops, the Latin American church did not go to the council as a pacesetter. It went rather as a learner.

The council was a vast learning experience for the Latin American church. The learning began with the bishops and their advisors and spread to grassroots levels through the ensuing years, resulting in a whole series of initiatives already alluded to and culminating in the Medellín conference in 1968.

The council convened every fall in Rome and continued for three and a half months. The experience of the council was particularly intense and stimulating for the bishops from Latin America, who had so much catching-up to do. But behind the scenes was a group probably more important in the life of the Latin American church—the *periti* and advisors. Many of them were young priests who had recently completed their studies, often in Europe. They acted as intellectual bridges for the Latin American church, interpreting what was taking place in council discussions and eventually reinterpreting for Latin America the ideological thrust of the council.

Much of the rest of the time before and after the sessions in Rome was also spent in learning sessions. Throughout Latin America or in Italy, preceding council sessions, groups such as Father Riccardo Lombardi's Better World Movement held numerous seminars or conferences that amounted to briefing sessions for church leadership groups in Latin America.

The council was important, too, for the formation of informal networks of the new ecclesial leadership groups. Ties were made or strengthened across continental lines, to the extent that Father Louis Colonnese from the U.S.A. was invited to the council as a *peritus* for Latin American bishops. Ties were also made across denominational lines, ties that continue twenty years later. (It is no accident that Protestant theologian Robert McAfee Brown has remained closely attuned to what is taking place intellectually south of the Rio Grande following his participation in Vatican II.)

But the ties that proved to be the most telling in the immediate history of the Latin American church were those forged among the Latin American bishops themselves. The four-year experience of the council brought them together in a way that no other experience had. In fact, CELAM was a weak instrument for change until the experience of Vatican II. At the heart of the Latin American groups was Bishop Manuel Larraín of Chile. A consummate integrator, he worked during the council to pull the Latin American church together and to project it into the future, or at least out of the eighteenth century.

CELAM met in Rome each year during the council sessions to hold its ordinary (yearly) conferences. Larraín was elected president in 1963, the second year of the council. He formed the idea of having a Latin American conference apply what was being expressed at Vatican II to the Latin American situation. At the psychologically appropriate moment, Larraín proposed this to other Latin American bishops at the last session of the council (1965). The idea was enthusiastically received by the other bishops and Pope Paul VI.

Vatican Council II was a modern plan for renewal of the universal church to which the Latin American church actively responded. The bishops realized that their next step would be the application of Vatican II to the Latin American situation. Thus the Latin American Episcopal Council convoked the Medellín (1968) and Puebla (1979) conferences. The Latin American church was moving on a sure path toward change.

2

A New Church:
From Medellín to Puebla

The church of silence is what observers dubbed the Latin American church at Vatican Council II. The relative lack of impact by the largest regional church in the world was a poor harbinger of what was to take place three years later at the CELAM conference at Medellín. Indeed few, inside or outside the church, were prepared for what was to happen at Medellín. The progressive document (more progressive than Vatican II) of the Medellín conference was very much out of step with a church that seemed not to have changed much in almost five hundred years.

For many in the church, 1966, the year after Vatican II, was a time to catch up on work long overdue at home and also a period in which to catch one's breath. The prolonged and intense efforts of a year of preparation and four years of involvement in the council left most participants temporarily exhausted.

Then, toward the end of 1966, the two-year process of preparation for the Medellín conference began. These preparations were often hidden from the view of those who did not take part directly. Moreover, because of the vastness of the region and the inferior quality of communication across national lines, it was difficult to comprehend all aspects of what was taking place.

The key integrator of the Latin American church, Bishop

Larraín, died in an auto accident in early 1966. Nonetheless, the highest level of leadership of the Latin American church carried on his initiative with no loss of momentum. Later in 1966, at its tenth annual meeting and its first since Vatican II, CELAM turned to the discussion of the development and integration of Latin America. The bishops made a pivotal decision that, although seemingly of little consequence, set a new direction for the forthcoming extraordinary conference at Medellín. In contrast to the ineffectual first extraordinary conference at Rio, which had canonical representation (delegates from each ecclesiastical region), Medellín would have pastoral representation (delegates from functional or apostolic sectors). The decision was crucial: it meant that the church would be analyzed and defined from the bottom up. No wonder, then, that Norman Gall writing on the church shortly after the Medellín conference would describe it as the "people of God" rather than the "hierarchy of God."[1]

The same CELAM meeting brought another structural change of note: the conference would use a now famous methodology that would follow the trinomial of the Vatican Council *Gaudium et Spes* (The Church in the Modern World): facts/reflection/recommendations. The change in methodology was monumental: it represented a shift from a perspective that was dogmatic, deductive and top-to-bottom to one that was exploratory, inductive, and bottom-to-top. If nothing more than this structural change had been made, a giant step would have been taken. In fact, much more advancement than just methodological would be achieved.

During the two years of preparation, small conferences, workshops, and think-tank sessions worked on the changes that the Medellín conference would reflect. Those who took part in the preparatory steps and in the conference itself recalled later the euphoria they experienced in the days of building something new. New leadership networks were the dynamo that made the enterprise energetic and productive. Their members ensured that changes would take place at Medellín.

The standard interpretation of what the conference achieved is that it applied Vatican II to Latin America. This would be a major achievement, one that no other regional church attempted. Nonetheless, Oliveros and others argue that what took place at Medellín was an interpretation of Vatican II in the light of the Latin American situation—rather than simply an application.[2]

The conference went beyond Vatican II. It broke new theological and ideological ground. The rest of this book elaborates that view.

Assimilating Vatican II

What was taking place in the period from the end of Vatican II to the Medellín meeting was a twin process of assimilation (of Vatican II) and Latinamericanization (the process of reflecting on the human and religious situation in Latin America and interpreting that situation in the light of Vatican II). Theologians assiduously studied the "new" theology expressed at Vatican II. Social scientists took on the task of the description and analysis of the Latin American situation. The processes acted as new engines for a balky old freighter. At first the ship moved rather uncertainly, but then, with the shedding of barnacles and with new energy sources, it sailed steadily on course.

The process of assimilating Vatican II began slowly with the commencement of the council meetings in 1962. At first the communication to Latin America of what was taking place in Rome was spotty and thin. The inability on the part of bishops and *periti* to share fully what was taking place at the council was due in part to theological ignorance.

In retrospect, too, one can sense that the Latin American bishops and many of their advisors suffered cultural shock, and understandably so. Many of the questions being discussed by the council were not "their" questions or at least not issues addressed in a way that would have been pertinent to Latin America. In many ways Vatican II witnessed a clash of cultures. The Europeans (and to a lesser degree participants from other developed countries) won the conflict. It was not an explicitly conscious conflict but it was real. European bishops and experts led the council in the direction of European interests. The central theme and the motivation of John XXIII in calling the council was aggiornamento. For the church of the developed world and European civilization, this meant bringing the church up to date about its place in the modern (European) world. Specifically, it meant addressing questions of faith or lack of it in a scientific age.

Aggiornamento would eventually mean something very different in the Latin American situation. This became increasingly clear to the theological and pastoral experts as they prepared for the Medellín conference. In many ways Latinamericanization has been a wrenching process, one not completed by Medellín, although a good beginning was made there. It entailed the pain of a creative enterprise, intensified by coming after four arduous years at the council and by being under the gun of the forthcoming conference. More, it was an uprooting of the Latin Americans from their European theological soil, at least in part. It meant growing on their own, away from the parental trunk, though clearly remaining an offshoot. No longer could the Latin American church be content with derivative thought. It was a process similar to that of a young man thinking his own thoughts and making his own plans, though guided by teachers and parents.

The process of thinking their own thoughts also meant that Latin Americans had to turn away from (although usually not all the way) European theologians, some of whom had been their mentors. The Latin Americans removed heroes such as Johannes Metz (political theology) and Jürgen Moltmann (theology of hope) from the main niches of their theological pantheon. In turn, Europeans (with some exceptions, such as Edward Schillebeeckx) found it difficult to understand what the Latin Americans were saying, why former students had changed, and why they were so demanding.

At the time of the Vatican council, aggiornamento for many Latin American bishops meant a simpler process than it did at Medellín. Many of them perceived aggiornamento in terms of a request of the pope to bring the church up to date. Theirs was often a passive response, one of attempting to learn what to do and then of muddling through some kind of implementation.

As all social learning, the assimilation and implementation of Vatican II took place in Latin America at considerably varying rates. Vatican II had a strong effect almost immediately in such places as Chile and parts of Brazil, regional churches that had updated themselves before Vatican II. The council had a much more muted and indirect impact in other countries, such as Mexico. Only after Medellín and especially in preparing for and experiencing Puebla did the Mexican church begin to feel the fuller impact of the Vatican council. The reasons for the delayed effect will be discussed later.

In countries where Vatican II had a more immediate effect a large-scale effort of *difusión* began. *Difusión,* the dissemination of aggiornamento ideas on a massive scale, took shape in the last two years of the council and continued thereafter. In many countries thousands of small groups sprang into existence to find out what had happened at Vatican II and to reflect on what the council meant personally and for the world in which they lived. Often these groups were started spontaneously by persons curious about the new theology of the council or about new practices proposed, especially in worship.

Here a convergence occurred. The thousands of active members of Catholic Action and other lay movements became an instant audience for the teaching of Vatican II and for the theology that undergirded the conciliar deliberations. They and their chaplains rushed to obtain and to discuss booklets containing council documents or popular commentaries.

The meshing of "new" ideology and "old" movement did not always proceed smoothly, as we shall see in the case of Catholic Action and liberation theology. Many Catholic activists evaluated lay movements such as the *Cursillos de cristiandad* or the Legion of Mary as being out of step with Vatican II. They believed that the orientation of the Cursillo and the Legion to "delivering the lay person to the doorstep of the parish office" did not reflect what were supposed to be the new authority relationships within the church.

Because of the example of Vatican II, its exploratory attitude, and its use of sacred scripture in a "new" way, many biblical study groups came into existence. Popular and inexpensive Spanish versions of the Bible appeared as part of this biblical movement. Millions of copies of the Bible were sold or distributed in the years after Vatican II.

Catholics in a number of places experienced another novelty: they began to learn about themselves and their church in the company of Protestants. This seemed to happen overnight in some places; elsewhere it has still not happened. But a general trend of openness to other religions had begun.

Few places reflect better the assimilation of Vatican II, the learning process that had begun, and the changes that have taken place, than the bookstore Librería San Pablo. The Paulinas, a community of sisters dedicated to the printing and dissemination of Catholic teaching, run the bookstore in midtown La Paz. Before Vatican II had much impact, the bookstore resembled a garden of pious books and devotional statues. Slowly the store began to change. First came council documents, then cautious commentaries often written by old-school Spanish or Italian seminary professors attempting to show how the council was in conformity with past teaching. Before long, the demand for the new theollogians, the masterminds of the council—Yves Congar, Karl Rahner, Edward Schillebeeckx, Hans Küng, Henri de Lubac—could hardly be met. Within another year appeared commentaries by Protestants favorable to the council, and then simply books by Protestants. Prospective readers often did not know a writer's background, nor did it matter to them. The Librería San Pablo moved into new quarters for its now large selection of contemporary books and publications.

Besides being a symbol of the progressive, open-minded, and ecumenical aspects of the process of assimilation that was taking place, the bookstore also reflected the small, middle-class, elitist stage of social learning taking place in the church. Some fifty miles away, Bishop Adhemar Ezquivel and his team were preparing rural Amerindians to become church leaders through study of Vatican II. In general, though, for most persons at the grassroots in the late 1960s, the impact of Vatican II was very slight.

In contrast with the United States where many religious publishing houses went out of business or were absorbed by secular houses, religious book and magazine publishing in or for Latin America has boomed. Chicago, with the largest Catholic population of any diocese in the U.S.A., no longer supports a Catholic bookstore in the Loop. Mexico City has several Catholic bookstores in the Zócolo area and supports one of the largest religious bookstores in the world, Librería Parroquial. The latter resembles a department store, with three floors of books and thousands of titles.

Latinamericanization

The other process facing the church, that of interpreting Vatican II from the viewpoint of the Latin American situation, was more complex, because it was more original than the process of assimilation. Two major interacting tasks were called for: first, a realistic analysis and delineation of the human and religious situation in Latin America and, second a theological reinterpretation, the creation of a Latin American theology in the light of Vatican II. Neither were easy tasks. The remainder of this chapter and the following chapter enlarge on the results or lack of results of these two tasks.

As is often the case, the task called for by higher administrators already was being attended to by entrepreneurs in the field. Two distinct groups had begun work on the analysis of the human and religious situation of the region. The first of these can be described as development institutes—institutes dedicated to social and religious research, dissemination of research results, and, often, continuing adult education. These institutes drew their inspiration from diverse immediate sources but in general developed out of the same general rationale: the need for Christian involvement in the world (that is, local and national development) and, along with it, the need for facts and for the analysis of causes of local and national situations, both social and religious.

Three of the main sources of inspiration for the institutes were François Houtart of Louvain University, French Dominican Louis Joseph Lebret, and the Society of Jesus. Houtart and his collaborator Emile Pin were among the first in the field. Houtart first helped to set up centers for socio-religious research in Bogotá and Rio de Janeiro. Then as more centers were started (although not always through Houtart) he created a formal network: FERES (Federation of Religious and Social Studies). FERES became increasingly transnational with a Latin American branch anchored by the Bogotá and Rio centers. Louvain functioned as the center of the network, coordinating information, urging what its field consultants perceived as needed lines of research, and obtaining from time to time money and personnel for collaborative studies.

One of the first of these projects, a very ambitious one, took place in the early 1960s. FERES undertook historical and "sociographical" studies of each Latin American country and church, together with studies on specialized themes, such as the clergy. On the Latin American side, Gustavo Pérez Ramírez and Alfonso Gregory coordinated the massive effort, which was done with limited resources. FERES efficiently published the results in a series of paperbacks and widely distributed them throughout Latin America.

The studies were rather superficial reports that repeated facts familiar to most historians and social scientists. They were almost devoid of analysis. Thus they are not remarkable as landmark case studies. But they were important for other reasons. First, they brought together a number of isolated facts that tended to escape the attention of church administrators and pastoral workers. Secondly, up to that time in Latin America, it was not common to pay more attention to "facts" than to predigested theory. Thirdly, the church was beginning to tell the truth about itself and the series helped put together a picture that was clear in some of its outlines, if blurry in detail. It was the first attempt of the Latin American church to make use of social science, and the effort widened the vision of many bishops.

Until 1962 most bishops in Latin America experienced isolation from other bishops and from the larger church organization to a degree unknown in the United States since the Civil War. Only rarely did the bishops meet within their own countries, and then only for episodic, ad hoc crises. Moreover, even in their own dioceses, bishops remained isolated in their see cities. They lacked resources and a pastoral vision that would lead them out to the countryside or into the neighborhoods of provincial capitals. Instead they acted out the cultural role of the *patrón* receiving his *clientes,* a cultural pattern familiar for more than four hundred years. Many bishops seldom or never ventured out of their see cities, except for occasional visits to the national capital. Up to the early 1960s, no one in a remote diocese in Peru could recall a bishop ever visiting a parish outside the city, despite the fact that the vast majority of Catholics resided in the countryside.

Thus, up to Vatican II most bishops possessed a vision of the church that was largely limited to their own dioceses and, at that, to one city. They contented themselves with selective reports from other parts of their jurisdiction. Hence, the use even of primitive sociological or historical materials that developed a larger sense of the national church or of the Latin American church represented a major advance.

Although Latin American bishops differed notably from bishops in the developed world in their isolation and lack of national organizational structures, nonetheless the Latin American modus operandi gave the bishops an advantage over their North American or European counterparts. Latin American bishops spent much of their day "receiving" persons, most of them ordinary citizens with a variety of problems. This contact has given many Latin American bishops a sense of the people that is lacking in many bishops of the developed world.

This sense of people, even though sometimes shaped on the skew toward the pious and dependent, helps to explain the relatively ready acceptance at Medellín and the reaffirmation at Puebla of the Latin American bishops' preferential option for the poor in pastoral planning. The much lower percentage of the poor and the relative structural isolation from the poor make such an option relatively unthinkable in the U.S.A. or Europe. The contrast between North America and Latin America emphasizes the impact of differences in structured interactions of bishops and laity.

Louis Joseph Lebret and his collaborators were most active in Uruguay, Argentina, and Bolivia. Paul Ramlot, Lebret's representative in Latin America, established the Centro de Economía y Humanismo (Center for Economy and Humanism) in Montevideo, and later IEPAL (Institute of Political Studies for Latin America) in Buenos Aires. North American Dominicans, loosely following Lebret's lead, founded IBEAS (Bolivian Institute for Social Study and Action) in La Paz.

The Jesuits, best known in Latin America for prestigious high schools and universities, began in the 1960s to emphasize social study and action centers on a typically comprehensive basis. Word came down through the ranks that the Jesuits should establish in each Latin American country a CIAS (Center for Social Investigation and Action). This general directive took on some variation from country to country but the commitment to social study and action was clear and steady. In countries where a center similar in conception to CIAS was already established, the Jesuits joined in collaborative effort, as Pedro Negre did at IBEAS. The CIAS idea was sometimes tailored to fit already existing structures within established universities, such as the Centro Bellarmino in Santiago, the grandfather of social research and action centers in Latin America.

The Jesuits also established notable specialized institutes that drew on the CIAS idea. In two of them—CEE (Center for Educational Studies) in Mexico City, and CIE (Center for Educational Investigation) in Buenos Aires—Jesuit researchers and collaborators researched and published widely on the place of education in society. At the grassroots level in Bolivia, Jesuit Javier Albó, with the help of others, established CIPCA, a center for the study and promotion of Aymara Indian culture.

The CIAS idea was important to the Jesuits and to the Latin American church for a variety of reasons. A number of the more talented, younger Latin American Jesuits went off to major universities, usually outside Latin America, to obtain advanced degrees in social science or education. Many of them later assumed leadership within the social science enterprise, government circles (as in Nicaragua), the theology of liberation, or church administration.

More importantly, the CIAS model led the Jesuits away from merely academic concerns to emphasis on social problems. This major shift has had important consequences for the Jesuits and for Latin American society. Nowhere is this more evident than in Paraguay or in Central America where Jesuit social commentators and activists helped the church confront manifestly unjust social structures. In Paraguay and El Salvador the Jesuits as a group have been threatened with mass expulsion or murder. They withstood the challenge but at the cost of individual exile or assassination.

With the mushrooming of social research and action centers, FERES was able to create a network of centers throughout most of Latin America. From initiatives of those centers and from collaborative research, a clearer and clearer view of the human and religious situation in Latin America emerged. But the description of the region from the accumulation of statistics led to more and deeper questions. Why was Latin America underdeveloped? Why were so many millions pushed to or kept at the margins of society?[3] A crisis was occurring within the social sciences in Latin America, especially within sociology and economics departments in universities. The crisis had to do with trying to explain Latin American underdevelopment.

The "development" model was proposed for Latin America and the Third World because of the success of the reconstruction

of Europe and Japan through the Marshall Plan. The U.S.A. in
the late 1950s and the 1960s turned much of its attention to Latin
America, in part to keep the western hemisphere free of communism. Scores of experts, including military advisors, and ship-
ments of goods, including large amounts of military supplies,
descended on Latin America under Point Four of the Marshall
Plan and military assistance agreements. Because the Marshall
Plan had worked so successfully with former enemies, why not
apply essentially the same plan to friends to the south?

U.N. Secretary General U Thant and President John Kennedy
helped focus on the crisis. U Thant declared the 1960s a decade
of development; Kennedy helped to concretize the same ideas
of development for Latin America through the Alliance for
Progress. After initial enthusiasm expressed by Latin Americans at the Punta del Este meeting that cemented the alliance,
disillusionment set in for Latin American economists and sociologists.

The Point Four plan was essentially flawed, as became apparent with the passing of years and with little of the progress that
had been evident in Europe and Japan. Planners turned to economists for new insights. Pioneers among the economists, such as
Theodore Schultz at the University of Chicago, began to focus on
the idea of human resources. The difference, they said, between
Germany/Japan and Latin America was the human resources
that had made recovery relatively simple in Germany and Japan,
given large amounts of capital. Latin America needed education
and training: that would lead to a sufficient level of human resources. Then, with capital infusion, the countries would begin to
"take off," to use Walt Rostow's term.

Import substitution through domestic industrialization became
another key theme of planners. International banks and monetary funds were set up to assist in this process. The Inter-
American Development Bank, the World Bank, and the
International Monetary Fund (IMF) soon had a strong hand on
the helm. Large private-sector banks, especially from the U.S.A.,
also made their way south. Their branch offices grew up all over
Latin America. These banks soon were filling their U.S. headquarters with Latin American profits in a way never dreamed possible. Especially Citicorp, Bank America, and Chase Manhattan

received increasingly substantial profits from their Latin American operations.

Not long after the U.S. Agency for International Development (AID) and Latin American governments drew up the basic game plan for Latin America through the Alliance for Progress, many Latin American economists and social scientists began their own analyses of the development plan. In brief, they became convinced that any development that took place would be _dependent_ development. Economic progress of their countries would take place especially to the profit of the developed world. This was so because the developed countries bought raw materials from Latin America at low prices and then sold it manufactured goods at a handsome profit. Later, as domestic industrialization took place, multinational companies of the developed world would move into the process and send profits back home.

The kind of development that many Latin American analysts saw taking place was uneven and inequitable. Certain sectors of Latin American society benefited (sometimes mightily) from economic progress, and other sectors fell further behind. The poor would get poorer, they said. And they were right.

The force of this early formulation of the dependency argument was not lost on young political activists who joined the discussion more fully in their university years. Nor was the argument lost on the Latin American church (though it took longer for the church, which had only recently joined discussion with social scientists and acquired a sense of the question). Nonetheless, within the two-year period of formal preparation for the Medellín conference, the Latin American church at its core (that of progressive experts and the bishops who listened to them) understood the dependency argument and stood ready to promote it at Medellín.

Another convergence thus occurred, this time between theologians and social scientists. And it occurred at precisely the time when sociologists and economists were focusing on the fact of *dependencia*. Increasingly thereafter documents written in preparation for the Medellín conference incorporated *dependencia* in their analysis. (The dependency argument presented here reflects its formulations in the late 1960s. The argument has since advanced through additional elaboration.)

The pace of social understanding, of evolution of positions within the church, would stun observers. When a CELAM preparatory meeting at Mar de Plata, Argentina, in 1966 discussed development and integration in Latin America, the group did so in traditional terms, those similar to ones used by the World Bank or the Alliance for Progress. By the time of a CELAM preparatory meeting at Itapoan Bahía, Brazil, in May 1968, the analysis was beginning to take a new turn. For one thing, the church was now talking about itself more actively than ever before—for example, in terms of "the presence of the church in the process of change in Latin America."[4] More, the Itapoan meeting incorporated the description and analysis of the socio-economic realities of Latin America as formulated by many Latin American economists and social scientists. The group took for granted the fact of dependence: "Underdevelopment in Latin America is the by-product of the capitalist development of the Western world." The Medellín conference would accept and enlarge on that line of analysis.

The first task in constructing a Latin American interpretation of Vatican II—analysis of the human and religious situation—was taking definite shape. The second task—a theological reinterpretation of Latin America, in effect the creation of a Latin American theology in the light of Vatican II—was also beginning. Based on social analysis, Latin American theology began to shape itself. Faced with domination and dependence, Latin American theologians turned to the theme of liberation. A new theology was taking shape.

Formal Preparations for Medellín

Each of the national churches was invited to have a hand in preparing for the Medellín conference. Questionnaires were sent out, some consultations were held, and the bishops discussed the forthcoming conference within their newly formed or newly strengthened national episcopal councils. But the most important preparations were taking place within the commissions and institutes formed by CELAM.

CELAM commissions and institutes began conducting consultations and study meetings to prepare for the writing of working documents. These meetings became the most important steps leading to the final Medellín document. Several meetings produced especially salient documents in terms of basic questions raised or of positions later taken. Of these the most important meetings took place at Baños, Ecuador, June 1966, on education, ministry, and social action; at Mar de Plata, October 1966, on development and integration of Latin America; at Buga, Colombia, February 1967, on the mission of the Catholic university in Latin America; at Melgar, Colombia, April 1968, on the missions; at Itapoan, 1968, a follow-up of the Mar de Plata meetings; and at Medellín, August 1968, on catechesis.

Experts were drawn from all over Latin America to produce *ponencias* (position papers) or to react to *ponencias* and then rewrite them into fuller working papers. Many experts were members of the new leadership networks mentioned earlier. To their numbers were added new members, experts in one field or another who had been working in their own national context somewhat isolated from the transnational networks. Thus those networks expanded and reshaped themselves for the purpose of influencing the outcome of the Medellín conference. Specialists from various fields and disciplines interacted in preparatory consultations. This widened and deepened the perspectives of the participants. The dynamics of their meetings were such that advances in theological and practical thinking were made rather easily. Many of the ideas emanating from Vatican II and from social analysis led the specialists to conclusions that were later taken for granted by Medellín participants who had taken part in preliminary consultations. In effect, the conference outcome was being determined even before the conference began.

None of the consultations mentioned dealt directly with theology, much less the theology of liberation. Yet theologians participated actively in the consultations and often acted as the principal writers of *ponencias*. Gustavo Gutiérrez, Eduardo Pironio, José Comblin, and others excelled at this type of activity. Thus theological and not simply organizational concerns were placed at the heart of the conference preparations. Theologians, though, had to focus their thoughts on practical affairs such as education, missions, and social action. It was theology done at the side of those immersed in practical activities—a considerable change from the theology that had typically been taught in Latin American schools of theology.

Prophets and Integrators at Work

Apart from formal CELAM consultations, a small group composed almost entirely of theologians was meeting to test and exchange ideas. Halfway through the four-year Vatican II period—March 1964—they met on Latin American soil, probably for the first time. To the quiet, picturesque university town of Petrópolis, Brazil, Monsignor Ivan Illich invited a select group of intellectuals for a meeting on Latin American theology.

In the U.S.A. Illich is best known for his ideas on the futility of schooling and for his broadsides on the medical profession. In 1964 Illich was the consummate leadership figure in Latin America. He oscillated between his roles as diagnostician and integrator. A Central European aristocrat, he became a New York City pastor, then head of two training schools for missionaries set up through funds from the U.S.A. at Petrópolis and at Cuernavaca, Mexico. Illich broadened the mandate given him and made the language schools into institutions with think-tank operations, replete with publication and documentation services.

Illich functioned well at bringing together "idea" persons, especially those with ideas similar to his own, which at the time ran along the line of radical latinamericanization of Latin American churches. The Petrópolis meeting took a giant step in that direction. Juan Luis Segundo, Gustavo Gutiérrez, and Lucio Gera presented probably the most influential position papers at the meeting. They opened the way toward a Latin American theology and expressed concerns that were to become richer, more systematic statements of liberation thought that began appearing four years later.

The inner circle that began at Petrópolis expanded through a series of informal meetings over the next four years. In 1965 alone, the group (which had flexible boundaries) met in June at Bogotá, and in July at Cuernavaca and Havana. Another pioneering network was being solidly established.

A further important network in the life of the Latin American church owed its inspiration to liberal Protestant churches and its financial resources mostly to outside sources, especially to the National Council of Churches (U.S.A.). ISAL (Church and Society in Latin America) began in Buenos Aires and Montevideo and branched out to the north and west. Eventually the movement became very influential, especially in Bolivia, where the majority of its members were Catholic priests or sisters.

Ecumenical cooperation became easier because the movement focused more on issues than it did on theology as such or on theological differences. The movement did include, however, a number of important Latin American theologians, especially Rubem Alves and Julio de Santa Ana (Protestants) and Hugo Assmann (Catholic). Richard Shaull, a Princeton theologian with longstanding contacts in Latin America, was influential at the beginning of the movement.

Some have seen in ISAL the importation of ideas that were largely North American, foreign to the real interests of Latin America. Thus the brooding concern about violence, which at times marked ISAL discussions, was thought to be drawn more from what was happening in the U.S.A. in response to the Vietnam crisis than from any realistic appraisal of the Latin American situation. In an interview Ivan Vallier concluded that ISAL meant little more than the funneling of money from pews in the U.S.A. into a revolutionary movement fueled with ideas from Princeton Seminary. (This was unfair to the Seminary.)

Crisis and Response in Latin America

Such an extreme interpretation has to be tempered by an understanding of what was taking place in Latin America in the 1960s. The idea of violence occurred to more than one Christian activist as a solution to a situation believed to be unjust. Their prototype was Father Camilo Torres. Torres joined a number of other Latin Americans, most notably Gustavo Gutiérrez, studying at Louvain University. Torres returned to Colombia in 1962 to become national chaplain to the university student movement. In 1966 he was killed by Colombian army bullets on his first armed foray as a guerrilla. For a few years his writings received considerable attention in Latin America and the U.S.A.

Three years after his death, a number of young activists and university students in Bolivia started guerrilla activity designed to bring down the government, in Teoponte, a village in the Los Yungas region, near La Paz. Like Torres, a number of the guerrillas joined the movement out of what they believed to be Christian motivation, convinced that revolution was the last recourse in working for a just society. Like Torres too, many of the guerrillas died in combat. (One of them was Néstor Paz, a man of considerable writing skill, who describes his thoughts on joining the movement in *My Life for My Friends.*[5])

The Teoponte movement was but one of the more romantic of the guerrilla movements that were being created in Latin America in the 1960s. Many of the movements employed FLN (National Liberation Front) or a similar title; almost always liberation was part of their self-designation. Among the movements, the best known for some time were the often boldly dramatic Tupumaros of Uruguay.

These groups drew their inspiration from a variety of founts that included a detailed knowledge of Mao Tse-tung's philosophy, or more commonly a vague desire for "socialism." Often groups could agree on neither ideology nor tactics. Nonetheless, two general influences affected them all. The first was Fidel Castro's overthrow of a very corrupt government. His small guerrilla movement was successful despite a large standing army and the pervasive presence of the U.S.A. in Cuba. Castro showed others that such efforts could work. (Those who followed such leads seldom stopped to analyze all the conditions, including widespread support by the church and the general populace, that brought Castro to power.)

Moreover, Castro showcased for Latin America a new form of government and social organization, one purporting to serve the common good and the interests of the people. Again, at least from a short distance, Fidel demonstrated to Latin Americans that there was another way to run a country. (The cost of so doing was seldom stressed, nor was the extensive dependence on the Soviet Union.)

The second general influence affecting many Latin Americans, and not just those inclined to violence, was the failure of the development model. The world economic system was seen to be organized in a way that benefited the developed world and left the Third World further and further behind.

With the military takeover of the Goulart regime in Brazil in

1964, the situation began to change for Latin American political life and for the Latin American church. After 1964 other Latin American countries found their presidential palaces occupied indefinitely by the military. The rules of the political game were beginning to change, and military juntas were dictating the changes. The situation continued for some years with almost daily reminders of church-military conflict in reports from such countries as El Salvador, Argentina, and Bolivia.

Final Preparations

By January 1968, only eight months remained before the conference, and persons charged with preparations had a sense of urgency that proved highly beneficial. Because of experience with Vatican Council II, they believed the bulk of the work of the conference had to be expressed in the preparatory documents if there were to be any breakthroughs, given the relatively short duration of the conference. Conference participants thus would ratify what had been prepared for them by the core group that began its work at Bogotá on January 19 in 1979. (The Puebla conference largely reversed the process of preparatory documents and ratification.)

Up to the beginning of 1968, CELAM headquarters had received or discussed only general principles or suggestions for the conference. Now was the time to begin careful delineation of themes. Forty-three bishops, experts, and assistants participated in the ten-day meeting at the Cristo Rey retreat center in Bogotá. They were, for the most part, CELAM insiders: bishops who were chief executives of CELAM and priests who were experts in theology, sociology, or some other field. Those who gathered for the meeting were moderates or progressives in theological or political orientation. The group included such bishops as Marcos McGrath, Avelar Brandão Vilela, Eduardo Pironio, Lucien Metzinger, Leonidas Proaño, and Cándido Padín. The group also included richly talented persons from CELAM headquarters who worked behind the scenes at the Medellín conference and for the four years to follow. They knew one another and cooperated easily, a major change from the days preceding Vatican II.

The group started its work at the very first full plenary session when three experts, including Gustavo Gutiérrez, presented their working papers. In effect these papers mapped out the major concerns of the forthcoming conference. After that the group broke up into smaller sections to enlarge on their working papers and to compose the preliminary working document. Looking back, one can discern the outlines of the work of the sixteen commissions of the Medellín conference. The preliminary working documents would contain the main characteristics of the final Medellín document.

Within weeks the preliminary working document was sent out to national episcopal conferences for their reactions. These conferences in turn invited comments from experts or interested parties in their own countries. Consultation tended to be limited to informed persons; consultation with the grassroots was virtually nil. In their national meetings, some episcopal conferences took up the document very systematically, whereas other episcopal conferences went over the document only routinely and without much psychological engagement.

After the Bogotá meeting, which produced the working document, came the formal convening of the Medellín conference by Paul VI. With that step taken, the sending of invitations to the conference was in order.

One of the great innovations of the conference was the inviting of non-Catholic observer-delegates. The initiative came from the newly created CELAM Department of Ecumenism with its headquarters in Buenos Aires, at once the site of a largely conservative church but also a place where Protestant and Jewish communities were strong. At first it was the intention of the Roman Commission for Latin America to limit the participation of non-Catholics to the plenary sessions, but as it turned out the non-Catholic observer-delegates were authorized to participate in all sessions. Their presence proved to be highly beneficial for the proceedings and brought ecumenism in Latin America to an entirely new level.

By the beginning of May, it became clear that Paul VI himself would be coming to Colombia to inaugurate the conference (although there was some hesitation later due to the wave of assassinations taking place throughout the world that year). The press was captivated by the idea of a pope going for the first time to

Latin America. Indeed the press was more interested in the person
of Pope Paul than it was in the conference.

The pope's journey was one more unusual event in an unusual
year. That year brought upheavals at universities in the U.S.A.
and elsewhere, the assassinations of Robert Kennedy and Martin
Luther King, Jr., the invasion of Czechoslovakia, the riotous
Democratic convention in Chicago, escalation of the Vietnam
War, the Cultural Revolution in China, and a military revolution
in Peru.

A year before his arrival, Paul issued an encyclical of great
significance to those involved with social justice issues: *Populorum Progressio.* It raised many questions about the justice of the
international economic system and created a climate of high expectation. Paul's interpretation of the modern economic situation paralleled many descriptions and analyses expressed later at
the Medellín conference. Nonetheless Paul's visit created some
apprehension and skepticism among those who were actively attempting to reshape the church in Latin America. Paul and the
Vatican were seen as advocates of gradualism (the "two steps
forward and one step back" formula familiar to anyone who has
worked in a large-scale organization).

Increased spates of unrest marked Latin America that year. In
addition to events surrounding the new military government in
Brazil (a president more repressive than the previous one came to
power in 1967), the church became a target elsewhere. Archbishop Mario Casariego was thought to have been kidnaped and
eventually released in Guatemala. None of the events was serious
enough to cancel the pope's visit or the holding of the conference
but they did foreshadow a pattern of violence and repression that
would become more systematic and widespread in the coming
years.

Despite external difficulties and a sense of apprehension, other
signs of what was to take place at Medellín promised a conference
that would be more forward-thrusting than any other event in the
life of the Latin American church. One such sign was that provided by Roger Schutz, prior of a Protestant religious community
in Taizé, France. After he was invited to the conference, Schutz
replied that he would arrive with a million Bibles in Spanish, to be
followed later by a half million in Portuguese. The Bibles had

been the work of an ecumenical team of scholars. Schutz also requested housing among the poor; he was to become a strong advocate at the conference for the church to stand at the side of the poor. So great is Schutz's standing now among the Latin American bishops that they gave him a standing reception at the Puebla conference.

Signals were being given off in Rome too that something special was to take place at Medellín. One of the dedicated Vatican-watchers at the time, Robert Graham, wrote two months before the Medellín conference: "The Vatican is now confident that the groundwork laid at this meeting will make of the conference the beginning of a new phase in the life of the church."[6]

The Medellín Conference

At the time, the four-day presence of Paul VI was a great occasion for the Latin American church. But the details of his visit and indeed his addresses are now largely forgotten. With Paul's departure, the conference participants settled down to two weeks of intense activity. The immensity of the work—writing a major statement about a large-scale institution in a vast and complex environment—quickly became apparent.

The direction the conference would take was set in the opening days of the meeting by a sociological overview and by *ponencias* on the major conference themes.[7] The "Sociography of the Continent" showed the participants a stark and realistic picture of the social and religious situation in Latin America. "The situation was much worse than we thought," bishops recalled later. From the beginning, then, the conference kept its feet on the ground. Further, the presentation created a climate of interest in and preoccupation with "temporal" themes, as Hernán Parada was later to remark.[8] He also pointed out that beginning this way kept the spirit of Vatican II alive and present. The conference was off to a flying start.

The seven *ponencias,* especially that of Pironio, ensured the theological depth of the document that the conference would issue.[9] They were well conceived and elegantly phrased. They dealt especially with the signs of the times: a continent marked by change and by institutionalized violence. After discussion of the *ponencias* the participants went on to write various versions of the conference conclusions. The final document would say, in brief, that the church is a sinful church in a sinful (unjust) society, one marked by structured inequalities. Latin America, it went on, is a region suffering from two massive evils: external dominance and internal colonialism.[10] Change was obviously called for and the church wished to take part in the change. The church chose the side of the poor. It must reach out to them, and to the whole continent. This would be accomplished through evangelization and lay participation (*pastoral de conjunto*) from which grass-roots communities (*comunidades de base*) would emerge.

In the face of such a situation, the participants called for liberation:

> Because all liberation is an anticipation of the complete redemption of Christ, the Church in Latin America is particularly in favor of all educational efforts which tend to free our people. . . . A deafening cry pours from the throats of millions of men, asking their pastors for a liberation that reaches them from nowhere else.[11]

When reflecting on the situation of institutionalized injustice in Latin America, the bishops at the Medellín conference agreed that the church had to choose sides. They chose the side of the poor and oppressed. Even though this would lead to the loss of support of the traditional elites, including the military, the conference participants felt that the commitment had to be made. It was, in their words, a gospel imperative. Moreover, a commitment to a horizontal, rather than a vertical, church, had to be made: during the days of Vatican II it had become clear that a communal ordering of the church was called for to bring it in line with the original mandate of Christ to his apostles. The methodology of the conference, of first presenting facts and then proceeding to scriptural and theological reflection, brought the bishops to a clear understanding of the necessity for change and commitment in a way that had never taken place before.

However, the Medellín participants did not write universally strong statements. Of the sixteen sections of the *Conclusions,* only three made a strong impact. The rest of the sections were mostly throwaways—unimaginative statements typical of international meetings. But the three on justice, peace, and poverty acquired a life of their own in the years to come.

Reactions to the conference document varied. The Vatican approved the document and made mention of its historical importance. Paul VI confided to Eduardo Pironio, then secretary general of CELAM: "The Latin American church had arrived at a degree of maturity and an extraordinary equilibrium that made it capable of assuming fully its own responsibility."[12] The Latin American stepchild had arrived at a maturity that had eluded it for almost five hundred years.

Other reactions, predictably, were not favorable. The document especially offended conservatives inside and outside the church. Some, of course, simply chose to ignore the document. But for many, Medellín set the Latin American church firmly on the course of Vatican II. Creative, change-minded groups in the church found in the document the inspiration they needed. The longtime observer for *Le Monde,* Henri Fesquet was to write: "Younger members of the clergy and militant lay persons found in the better passages of the conference *Conclusions* new motives for continuing their struggle and for putting up better with isolation and misunderstanding."[13]

In sum, a new ideology for the Latin American church had been born. Progressive thinkers had assumed intellectual leadership of the church and set it on a new course of change. The highest church leadership in Latin America endorsed an ideology that would become increasingly clarified and elaborated as the theology of liberation in the coming years. The shift from development to liberation, with spiritual as well as material overtones, had been made. The most important event in the modern era of the Latin American church had taken place.

The conference was not only to open a new course to the theology of liberation; it was also to express the rationale for a new church community, to open further the way for expressive movements such as the charismatic, and to put ecumenical dialogue on a new level. The conference fostered an unprecedented emergence of the laity, such as is still largely unknown in the U.S.A., Canada, or Europe.

These were major achievements of the conference. But the

church at Medellín made a serious omission, one for which it would pay dearly in years to come. Medellín did not consider what effect the changes it was proposing would have on the social climate in which it had to operate. Many individuals and institutions would have to make adjustments to new modi operandi proposed by the church. The church did not consider what its proposed changes would mean to other political entities. And more seriously, it did not delineate a policy of dealing with the changing political environment, in which the military was becoming increasingly a major political force. The church and the military set themselves on collision course, and church navigators, with very few exceptions, did not foresee the shoals and suffering that lay ahead.

From Medellín to Puebla

When the 130 bishops approved the sections of the final document of the Medellín conference, they did so overwhelmingly: negative votes never exceeded five. Nevertheless, some bishops and other participants had reservations about the final document—indeed, about the whole direction that the conference had taken. Reactions to the conference confirmed their hesitations: persons on all sides wondered about the changes that the Latin American church proposed.

Conflict and division were to dog the church in the years to follow.[14] The conflict of viewpoints was to continue eleven years later in the meeting halls of the Puebla conference. The ensuing debate largely centered on whether the church should be involved actively in the social, political, and economic process of change that was taking place in Latin America or whether it should limit itself to "spiritual" values. Some obviously hoped to lead the church back to where it had been before the Medellín conference.

Despite conflicts, the eleven-year period between Medellín and Puebla were filled with major achievements for the Latin American church. However, these achievements should not be allowed to mask the fact that large sections of the church changed only very gradually. Many, clerical and lay, were psychologically incapable of rapid changes. Years of training and practice in one orientation would not suddenly be reversed. Years passed before changes would become evident in some places, such as parts of Mexico and Colombia. But the important factor in the Latin American church was that change was made legitimate. Many were to seize on that legitimacy to promote changes in ideology and practice.

The changes also had a beneficial effect on relationships with the historical Protestant and Jewish communities. Observer-participants noted from the start the change in atmosphere at the Medellín conference. At the last liturgy of the conference, Colombian television viewers watched with some amazement as five non-Catholic participants approached and received communion. When inquiries were made by the press, Archbishop Botero Salazar of Medellín responded, "It was something that was required, given the atmosphere of fellowship and participation."[15]

CELAM executives and staff members worked diligently for the four years following the Medellín conference to make known the implications of the conference. They published extensively, sponsored regional seminars, and enhanced the activities of CELAM institutes. However, after 1972 the progressive direction of the *Celamistas* largely ended and new personnel began to pursue a more cautious, spiritualizing tendency. The election of conservative Archbishop Alfonso López Trujillo as secretary general brought about this shift.

CELAM became increasingly less important to the spearheading groups that were guiding the church in the direction of change. The strongest networks of Christian activists were now being formed nationally. They did not involve violence, as had Camilo Torres or the Teoponte movement. They sprang up all over Latin America. The best known included ONIS (National Office of Information) in Peru, ISAL in Bolivia, the Priests for the Third World in Argentina, the Group of Eighty in Chile, and the Golconda movement in Colombia.[16]

At the same time, a much larger number of ad hoc groups appeared. Participants in these groups banded together over a single issue or event and then disbanded. Most groups issued formal statements of their positions. Local newspapers usually reprinted these statements, at least in countries where repression was less severe. Nationally and internationally, statements and position papers were passed from hand to hand and began to be collected by documentation centers. A number of the more salient and universally applicable statements appeared in collections reprinted in Latin America, the U.S.A., and Europe.[17]

Documentation centers became new major aspects of life in the church. They reflected much of what was happening in Latin America. Whereas activist elements in the church previously established development institutes dedicated to social and religious study, after the Medellín conference activists increasingly turned their energies to more direct action through national movements such as ONIS or ISAL, or through human rights activity as members of justice and peace commissions. These commissions sprang to life following the intensification of repression in Latin America, especially in the southern tier countries of South America and in much of Central America.

Communication of what was taking place at local and national levels and interchange of ideas among activists and theologians took place through established journals, mimeographed newsletters, or position papers. These publications crossed national lines and were collected in documentation centers. These centers were either national or regional; CRIE, for example, served as the ecumenical documentation center for Central America.

The centers became focal points where main issues facing the churches could be aired. They also became targets of hostile governments or right-wing forces. Publication of the "facts" in a repressive climate made the centers highly unpopular with repressive forces. This was true even in relatively free Mexico. Following the murder of Father Rodolfo Aguilar, who had been promoting mail and sewage services in slum areas, Mexican police sacked the office of CENCOS (Center for Social Communication), which had been documenting Aguilar's work, and attempted to intimidate the director of the center.

These centers are linked in an informal network promoted at an international meeting sponsored by the journal *Christus* in Mexico City. During the Puebla conference, CRIE furnished efficient clipping and documentation service, and CENCOS provided a convergence point for conference participants, theologians, activists, and journalists.

The Puebla Conference

The death of John Paul I and the delay caused by the election of John Paul II postponed the third extraordinary CELAM conference to January 1979. This conference would take place at the Palafoxiano Seminary at Puebla, Mexico. In 1978 groups working at CELAM headquarters began preparing for the conference.

At CELAM López Trujillo, with encouragement from Vatican officials, was very much in command. He carefully selected committee members and experts to compose the preliminary working document. They produced the "green book" (from its cover), divulging a cautious, otherworldly orientation, a perspective that had been largely put aside at Medellín. Clearly an attempt at setting back the bold positions taken at Medellín was afoot. Almost universally, the national episcopal conferences rejected the document as too timid, too general, and too spiritualizing. Most felt that the green book failed to address the urgent issues of the day for Latin America and the church.

In part the bishops reacted as they did because (in contrast to preparations for the Medellín conference) they consulted, on a wide scale, with grassroots organizations in preparation for Puebla. This was to be a different kind of a meeting from that at Medellín. Medellín was a conference controlled in large part by experts; Puebla was a conference controlled by the bishops. To be sure, the bishops were in contact with experts. But they assumed much greater leadership in the running of the Puebla conference. And there were more of them there, 191 (130 at Medellín). Their consulting with the grassroots and taking over the running of the conference would affect the rate of change in a number of Latin American churches. By and large Medellín influenced the Mexican church only minimally. Puebla had a much greater impact in Mexico and not simply because the conference took place within its borders. This time the Mexican bishops were strongly influenced by movements from below and by Mexican intellectual circles.

The change from charismatic to formal leadership is a natural evolution of change within an organization, and it was welcomed by the networks of experts who had been steering the church in that direction. Moreover, the same methodology that strongly influenced the outcome of the Medellín conference had a similar impact on the bishops and other participants at Puebla. They again began by considering the human and religious situation of Latin America, moved to biblical and theological reflection on the situation, and then proceeded to pastoral conclusions.

The description of the Latin American situation was as grim as it had been in 1968. In fact, the bishops in retrospect could see that the poor were getting poorer and new injustices in the form of enfringements of human rights had multiplied. But now the bishops saw more clearly the roots of the unjust situation:

a. We see the continuing operation of economic systems that do not regard the human being as the center of society, and that are not carrying out the profound changes needed to move toward a just society.

b. One of the serious consequences of the lack of integration among our nations is that we go before the world as small entities without any ability to push through negotiations in the concert of nations.

c. There is the fact of economic, technological, political, and cultural dependence; the presence of multinational conglomerates that often look after only their own interests at the expense of the welfare of the country that welcomes them in; and the drop in value of our raw materials as compared with the price of finished products we buy.

d. The arms race, the great crime of our time, is both the result and the cause of tensions between fellow countries. Because of it, enormous resources are being allotted for arms purchases instead of being employed to solve vital problems.

e. There is a lack of structural reforms in agriculture that adequately deal with specific realities and decisively attack the grave social and economic problems of the peasantry. Such problems include access to land and to resources that would enable them to improve their productivity and their marketing.

f. We see a crisis in moral values: public and private corruption; greed for exorbitant profit; venality; lack of real effort; the absence of any social sense of practical justice and solidarity; and the flight of capital resources and brain power. All these things prevent or undermine communion with God and brotherhood.

g. Finally, speaking as pastors and without trying to determine the technical character of these underlying roots, we ourselves see that at bottom there lies a mystery of sinfulness. This is evident when the human person, called to have dominion over the world, impregnates the mechanisms of society with materialistic values.[18]

Such analysis is this-worldly and antitriumphalistic, distinct changes in outlook in the Latin American church. Such a line of reasoning carries the church away from partnership with the status quo and also sets it against the military in some countries.

After this description and analysis of the human situation, the bishops began biblical and theological reflection. By 1979 the theology of liberation had achieved greater maturity, and it is thus represented in the Puebla document. The bishops defined much more fully than they had done at Medellín authentic, integral, and total liberation. The ideology of liberation undergirds their thinking.

The reception of John Paul II by the Mexican people exceeded by far the reception given earlier to Paul VI in Colombia. John Paul's visit also cemented a special relationship of the pope with Latin America, a relationship that intensified during a twelve-day visit to Brazil in mid-1980. No longer was Latin America the lost stepchild of Spain and Portugal. It was beginning to assume intellectual and moral leadership proportionate to its status as by far the most populous segment of the Catholic Church. In turn, John Paul understood that he must engage the Latin American church in discussion rather than continue the relative neglect the Vatican had contented itself with for centuries. John Paul had witnessed for himself the awakening of a giant.

The global perception of that awakening could be measured in part by the press corps that went to Mexico. The press office for the pope's visit to Mexico officially accredited some 2,200 journalists—more than came for the Olympics in 1968. Officials shook their heads. Earlier, when Paul VI had left Colombia before the Medellín conference, many of the press also departed; those who stayed on filed routine reports from the conference. The press office at the Puebla conference accredited some 3,200 journalists, and their reporting was hardly routine.

Puebla reaffirmed the direction taken at Medellín. There would be no turning back. Indeed, the bishops at Puebla went further. They more clearly and fully committed the church to the service of the poor and spoke of its preferential option for the poor and oppressed. They also took a more explicit and stronger stand for human rights. The experience of the years since the Medellín conference had taught the church new political and moral lessons.

Also evident at Puebla was a major shift from a hierarchical to a communal church. The Puebla document describes much more fully what that church would be. In contrast to rather vague discussion at Medellín about a *pastoral de conjunto* (clerical and lay participation), the bishops at Puebla developed in considerable detail their thoughts on grassroots Christian communities, the *comunidades de base*. Indicative of the shift, many representatives of grassroots communities were present at Puebla in person or through numerous statements communicated to the bishops. The bishops, too, faced the reality of some two million Catholics living in *comunidades de base* at the time of the Puebla conference. The church of promise at Medellín was becoming the church of fulfillment at Puebla.

Since the Puebla Conference, the Vatican through the Congregation for the Doctrine of the Faith has monitored closely the theologies of liberation. In August 1984 the Congregation through the initiative of Cardinal Joseph Ratzinger, its prefect, issued an "Instruction on Certain Aspects of the Theology of Liberation." Many observers of Latin American theology found that no major Latin American theologian holds the views singled out for warnings, while acknowledging that some activists uncritically propound what was criticized in the statement. Leonardo Boff and other theologians welcomed the document and look forward to what it promises: another document that will detail in positive fashion the richness of this theme of liberation.

3

A New Ideology:
The Theology of Liberation

When informed that the theology of liberation would be discussed at the next national meeting of the Catholic Theological Society of America, the president of that society replied that it was not a good idea: the fad would have blown away by the time of the convention. Andrew Greeley, another trend-spotter, thought worse—that liberation theology was a fraud, nothing but justification for violence. European theologians saw some good in liberation theology but wanted to spiritualize it. John Paul II on his way to Santo Domingo was quoted as saying that liberation theology was no theology at all.

To those who watched the theological scene in the United States in the late 1960s and through the 1970s, such comments were not unusual. They were heard about a variety of trends and movements. Every eighteen months a wave of enthusiasm for a "new" idea swept through theological schools and journals. Depending on when one entered the scene, one encountered Teilhard de Chardin on evolutionary thought, or Dietrich Bonhoeffer on discipleship, Harvey Cox on the secular city, Van Buren and Altizer on the death of God, Moltmann on hope, Metz on violence, or a variety of experts on Eastern Christianity. Fads that were purported to be theories remained in the theological consciousness as

partial insights or bad dreams. Five years after intense interest
was shown in the death of God "movement," Thomas Hamilton
was able to attract only a handful of persons to a session on the
subject at the annual meeting of the American Academy of Religion.

The fact is that theology of liberation is not a fad. It was conceived in the mid-1960s and is now a full-fledged adolescent with
adult intuitions and a strongly developing body. Despite gossip
from the right that the theology of liberation was condemned at
the Latin American bishops' meeting at Puebla in 1979, the ideology of liberation was reaffirmed by the bishops. John Paul II
himself used much the same sort of language in later speeches in
Mexico and Rome, and in his encyclical *Redemptor Hominis*.[1]

The creation of original religious thought in Latin America
came as a surprise to most North American and European intellectuals.[2] They had grown accustomed to seeing little but derivative religious or philosophical thought in Latin America. Latin
Americans either used translations of French or German, sometimes Dutch or Italian, works or they wrote their own manuals,
closely copying European models of thought.

Importance

The number of books and magazines contributing to the development of liberation thought continues to grow.[3] Orbis Books,
the major publisher of liberation thought in English, alone has
produced seventy volumes, and this for an audience mostly in the
U.S.A. and Canada. Paulo Freire's *Pedagogy of the Oppressed*
has gone through seventeen printings in English alone and is to be
found in bookstores in most prominent North American universities.[4] Gustavo Gutiérrez's *A Theology of Liberation* has sold over
65,000 copies in the U.S. edition.[5] Further, many North American
theological schools, Catholic and Protestant, routinely include
materials from liberation theology in their courses.

Latin American theology also has an ever stronger influence in
other Third World regions. There theologians have been encouraged to follow the lead of the Latin Americans and create
religious thought drawn from their own socio-cultural context.
Bonds, too, are being formed among theologians of the Third
World.[6]

In Latin America the theology of liberation furnishes an intellectual system that has been influencial at both the top and the
bottom. It has served in a loose way as the major intellectual system behind many of the national and regional church statements.
It took a more direct place center stage at the Puebla conference.
There it supplied many of the core ideas, especially those expressed in part two, on the content and implications of evangelization. But liberation thought has been used as well by many
(certainly not all) persons involved with grassroots Christian
communities, a topic that will be discussed in the next chapter.

For many in the Latin American church the theology of liberation is more than an academic intellectual system: it is their ideology. This ideology provides a worldview and leads to pastoral and
sometimes political consequences. It is an ideology in the technical sense of combining an intellectual system with values. The
theology of liberation proposes goals for society, and in doing so
becomes a distinct type of ideology.[7]

However, and this is important, for many, especially Latin
American bishops, liberation thought is not ideology in the usual
sense of the term. Yes, it is visionary thinking; its founders speak
explicitly about utopia. But it is not integrated assertions,
theories, and aims constituting a socio-political system.

Therein lies much of the difficulty outsiders experience about
liberation thought. The theology of liberation has an ontology, a
logic, a methodology, a psychology, and an ethic that serve as a
foundation for an ideology. But for most the theology of liberation does not have a socio-cultural program beyond preference
for a "third way" or for the "socialist" option. At Puebla many
of the bishops were saying, *"Ni capitalismo, ni comunismo."*
What then? "That is for others to say; we do not have a program;
we are not politicians or political scientists."

This aspect is important because, as we shall see, the match-up
between the ideology of the church and that of the military is quite
uneven. The military in many countries, because of its doctrine of
national security, has an integrated system of assertions, theories,
and aims that constitute a socio-cultural system. The church does
not.

Apart from the question of ideology, the theology of liberation
offers a vivid insight into the way that many Latin American
church-related persons think about the church and the world, the

way they reconstruct the world. That worldview may or may not be the "right" way to conceive reality but the thinking is a fact that others, especially political agents, have to deal with.

Thus, the shift in Latin American theology becomes a matter of importance to political elites, proponents of the status quo, the "marginalized" masses, and to transnational interests, especially multinational corporations and First World leaders, for the dominant ideology of the Latin American church is directed to macro-sociological concerns as well. Indeed, as currently taught, the theology of liberation is strongly opposed to what are perceived as the interests of North America, Europe, and Japan. The theology of liberation points an accusatory finger at the First World.

Anyone who wants to understand the theology of liberation should be aware of two cautions. First, liberation theology is not a monolithic Latin American theology. Given the vastness of the region, the difficulties in communication, and the rapid-breaking development of liberation thought, it is difficult for outsiders to know who among Latin American theologians are to be relied on as authentic representatives of liberation theology. Is José Comblin to be considered a theologian of liberation? Are the theologians of the liberation of the people (*pueblo*) to be numbered in the liberation camp? No, says historian of the theology of liberation, Mexican Jesuit Roberto Oliveros.[8] Indeed theologians of liberation find it increasingly necessary to define their position against other Latin Americans who do not fully share their views.

There are other currents of thought in Latin American theology and some, notably Comblin's thinking about the national security state, have influenced bishops and indeed other theologians. But the theology of liberation is by far the most influential and representative movement in Latin American religious thought. That is true for the historical Latin American Protestant churches as well as the Catholic Church.

The other caution is that liberation thought should not be reified beyond its true measure. It is obvious on reflection but worth repeating that the theology of liberation has not been internalized fully by church leaders or pastoral ministers, clerical or lay. Like all incomplete ideologies, theology of liberation is at times strongly unified and dynamic, but at other times parts of the doctrine become inoperative or are forgotten. Thus, Latin American liberationists pay considerably more attention to "external domination" by other countries than to "internal colonialism" within Latin America, though both evils have been condemned and they are seen as intertwined.

Origins

In their efforts to show that their theology is truly and thoroughly Latin American, some of the active originators or champions of liberation thought have been careful to point out that their theology is not conciliar (Vatican II), meaning not European, or even postconciliar in the sense of being an application of Vatican II. Their writings, especially that of Roberto Oliveros, give at times the impression that liberation theology owes no debts. But however distinct liberation theology may be from traditional theology, both Catholic and Protestant liberation theologies develop from some clearly identifiable sources.[9]

On the Catholic side, liberation theology was influenced heavily by the social teaching of the church commencing with Leo XIII, modern European theology, Vatican II, and the CELAM conference at Medellín. These are influences that lead some if not all current liberationists to where they are. The first three events or movements are closely related and at times appear to be seamless. The last, the Medellín conference, was as much influenced by liberation thought as that thought was influenced by it.

The phenomenon of modern Catholic social teaching is clearly identifiable but not always well understood. One source of misunderstanding is that readers, especially untrained theologians (including bishops), have tended to give the doctrine an absolute quality, much as they did to the arguments of medieval scholastic thought. But Catholic social teaching has evolved. Popes since Leo XIII have taken progressively wider or stronger stances on social and political issues. In fact, some of the later papal teaching contravenes or contradicts earlier teaching. Thus, Leo's statement that socialism must be "utterly rejected" was modified by later popes who saw values in the practice of socialism and in cooperation with socialists in the pursuit of social justice.

This misunderstanding of the evolutionary character of Catholic social thought leads astray those who rely on older positions. This is especially true of the military in Argentina, Brazil, and Chile. In those countries military ideologues incorporate a "Catholic integralism" into their military doctrines. These military doctrines not only cite positions taken from a European context of seventy or a hundred years ago but ignore the consistent and strong stands of the church against the excesses of capitalism.

What is called Catholic social teaching is found mainly in papal encyclicals and discourses. Much of the content of the teaching is not new: the fathers of the church and the great scholastics expounded most of the principles. It is generally agreed that "Catholic social doctrine" as a coherent modern enterprise begins with Leo XIII.[10]

Leo created a dramatic beginning for modern social teaching with the issuance of the first great social encyclical. Sensing the mood he was about to create, Leo entitled the encyclical *Rerum Novarum* ("of new things"). The encyclical created a sensation in 1891. Much of it reads as fairly tame now, although there still are some surprises, such as strong statements against the very rich.

Rerum Novarum pictured the socio-economic situation as one in which workers had been given over to the callousness of employers and the greed of competition. A few very rich have inordinate power over all the rest. Leo, though, rejects socialism as the solution. Of course, the socialism he had in mind does not embrace the myriad forms of socialism practiced in various countries today. Socialism is "utterly" rejected by Leo because private ownership accords with the law of nature.

Likewise, *Rerum Novarum* rejects class struggle: different classes are to live in harmony with one another. They who have money should give what they do not need to the poor. Leo sees this as a duty in charity rather than justice. This aspect of Catholic social teaching will grow much more pointed and forceful by the time of John XXIII and Paul VI. In contemporary social teaching one will find nothing like the statements of Leo about poverty and justice, such as: "In God's sight poverty is no disgrace. In fact, God calls the poor 'blessed.' Such reflections will keep the rich from pride and will cheer the afflicted, inclining the former to generosity and the latter to tranquil resignation."[11] Sentiments like that make contemporary theologians and activists wince. But there is nothing better than such statements to point out the evolutionary and dialectical character of modern social teaching. Its changing character confuses the uninitiated and can be manipulated to bolster reactionary opportunists, but the evolutionary and dialectical method will foreshadow the method and the exploratory character of liberation theology.

Leo's greatest achievement was probably his concern for distributive justice. He demanded that workers share in the benefits they helped to create. For the Carnegies, Mellons, Pullmans, and Krupps of the industrial world, this was revolutionary and unacceptable thinking. For the working class it became a rallying call that stimulated the drive to unionization, better working conditions, and a greater share in benefits, including pensions.

Leo's stand had its greatest effect in the United States and parts of Europe. The church stood clearly on the side of the working class. As late as the early 1950s there were twenty-eight U.S. labor institutes with formal ties to Catholic universities. A few labor movements of Catholic inspiration or participation appeared in Latin America, notably in Venezuela, Colombia, and Costa Rica. But Catholic social teaching remained virtually unknown in Latin America until the stirrings of Vatican II.

Pius XI issued the second great social encyclical, *Quadragesimo Anno*, on the fortieth anniversary of *Rerum Novarum*. He reinforced themes of *Rerum Novarum*, but 1931 furnished a somewhat new situation. It was the second year of the great depression. The concentration of wealth had become an even graver problem.

One senses the threat of the Russian revolution and the "menace of socialism" in Pius's encyclical. But, following the lead of English and German Catholic intellectuals, he also questions capitalism as a system. For one thing, he is much more sensitive than Leo to the question of private property. Right is not the same thing as use. And the right of ownership is not absolute. Thus, "a man's superfluous income is not entirely left to his own discretion."[12]

Pius strongly criticizes capitalists who make excessive profits and pay bare subsistence wages to their workers. Again Leo's theme of distributive justice appears, only this time the teaching is stronger and more concrete. Pius calls for just distribution of profits and for humane working conditions. He discusses the criteria for a just wage, a theme that would be explored for years by Catholic intellectuals in the U.S.A. and Europe. He encourages social legislation. Workers must be allowed to be free to join unions, though at the same time Pius warns that workers have obligations in justice and have no right to demand all the profits.

Many tend to forget or overlook the strength of Pius's criticism of capitalism. He finds too much wealth and economic domination in the hands of a few, giving them excess power. One sentence alone will give a sense of the depth of his conviction: "The whole of economic life has become hard, cruel, and relentless in a ghastly manner."[13]

With Pius XI, the position of the church on socialism begins to shift. Pius perceives that socialism has changed in the forty years since *Rerum Novarum*. The communistic form must be rejected but there is a "mitigated socialism" that has some affinity with the principles of Christianity. Third World theologians today carry the argument further and argue that some forms of socialism have greater affinity to the principles of Christianity than do any other known forms of political economy. But Pius was not ready for that. Instead, he says, "No one can be at the same time a sincere Catholic and a true socialist."[14] Nonetheless, the ecclesiastical perception of socialism is changing.

Pius anticipates liberation theology in another way. Probably for the first time the church sees sin as collectivized. In modern industrial life, injustice and fraud take place under "the common name of a corporate firm so that no one need take individual responsibility."[15] The Latin American bishops at Medellín and Puebla spoke forcefully about institutionalized injustices and collective sin. This represents a major shift in traditional Catholic (and Protestant Evangelical) thinking: Catholics almost uniformly refused to recognize anything more than individual injustice and sin.

One of the most vigorous advocates of the social teaching of the church was Pius XII, whose pontificate bridged the era from mid-depression to 1958. Yet one is hard pressed to isolate major statements. Only two of his encyclicals deal with social justice—*Summi Pontificatus* and *Mystici Corporis*—and they treat only selected aspects of it. Instead of the grand statement,

Pius XII was the master of frequent statements on important occasions. He made superlative use of modern communications within the papal framework. As one indication of the contributions that he made to modern social teaching, Guerry's *Social Doctrine of the Catholic Church* has some sixty references to Pius's teaching.[16]

Perhaps Pope Pius XII's major contribution was to delineate more clearly many aspects of the social teaching of the church and to lay the groundwork for John XXIII's and Paul VI's great social encyclicals. One of the areas that Pius XII elucidated more clearly was that of the social role of private property. Property is seen as playing a vital function for family and social life, as well as the more commonly emphasized personal role. The force of his teaching is shown by such statements as: "Whether serfdom comes from the power of private capital or from the state, the effect is the same."[17]

John XXIII brought new vigor to the scene with two major encyclicals and the convocation of Vatican II. All three events expressed a new self-understanding of the church and opened much wider horizons for the church-world thematic. John opened floodgates in the Latin American church. His teaching and that of Vatican II foreshadow the theology of liberation. Not only will the themes introduced by John and Vatican II be resumed by Latin American theologians, but a new methodology emerges, one that will become crucial for the efforts of liberation theologians.

John's encyclicals *Mater et Magistra* and *Pacem in Terris* (which was introduced at the United Nations) repeat familiar teaching about workers and unions. But John spoke also about the international order that was changing drastically. New nations were springing into being at the rate of practically three a year.

John spoke about just wages and strikes as did previous popes. But he also discussed economic aid, the use of farm surpluses at the international level, and in a forceful statement asked the well fed to look after the undernourished "without imperialistic aggrandizement." He called for the state to take a more active role, and even talked about state ownership. Many of the things he said sounded like favorable comments on distinctive features in some socialist countries. In *Pacem in Terris* there is no condemnation of communism or socialism. Indeed John distinguishes between philosophies and movements. Catholics and socialists, both striving for social justice, could meet and cooperate.

Persons in the Third World and in non-Catholic churches noted the change of tone in *Pacem in Terris*. The encyclical goes beyond the Catholic world; it addresses all Christians and all persons of good will. In so doing, John won the hearts of many—and raised the hackles of some conservatives and industrialists.

John also opened a new topic: he warned against colonialism and new forms of imperialism. Whatever implications there are for the developed countries remain to be discussed by the churches of the U.S.A. and Europe. By contrast, the church in Latin America has made colonialism and imperialism (dependency) central to its analysis.

Vatican II was the great event of the Catholic Church in the last four centuries. One may not agree with it, but one cannot ignore it. It has been seen by many theologians, Catholic and Protestant, as the church in the process of reforming itself. Social scientists would refer to the process as modernization, revitalization, adaptation, or organizational reform.

The process of reform was begun by describing carefully the situation of the church and that of the world. Then the council searched sacred scripture for the primitive or developed images it needed for itself and for its role in the world. Thus, the church no longer simply emphasized the hierarchical aspects of authority but returned to thinking of itself as "the people of God," "the common priesthood," a "royal nation"—all images of shared authority.

In the longest and most influential document of the council, *Gaudium et Spes* (The Church in the Modern World), a "new" methodology is introduced. Many theologians now believe that the methodology of *Gaudium et Spes* is every bit as important as its content. The methodology used in the document turns traditional theology on its head. Instead of proceeding in the time-honored fashion, discussing theological or biblical principles and then applying them to a present-day situation, *Gaudium et Spes* reverses the process: it begins with a careful analysis of the de facto situation, then turns to sacred scripture and theology for reflection on that situation, and finally, as a third step, makes pastoral applications. Theological reflection thus becomes the second, not the first, step.

Tradition, established theology, and the magisterium of the church had been used as the starting point in previous papal teaching, other Vatican II documents, and in traditional theology. *Gaudium et Spes* plunges right into the current world situation. It was almost the last of the schemata to be developed by the council. It proved to be the bridge into the future.

In the description of the church in the world, *Gaudium et Spes* makes use of social and behavioral sciences. Previously philosophy, the preferred "handmaiden," guided the theological enterprise. The church now searches the given socio-cultural situation for the "signs of the times," to hear the voice of God in them.

In *Gaudium et Spes* the church also returns to sacred scripture more directly than it was accustomed to doing. It thereby employs a more thorough hermeneutic—that is, a contemporary search for the meaning of the world and of world events in the light of the scriptures.

As far as content goes, in *Gaudium et Spes* the church again condemns strongly the concentration of wealth and power for the benefit of a few. The church also expands its teaching on private ownership. For North Americans, no point of the social teaching of the church is harder to grasp—or perhaps better said, no segment of that teaching is less known than that on private property.

The conciliar fathers at Vatican II said that the traditional right of private ownership needs to be balanced by the right inherent in various forms of public ownership. Moreover, a person's lawful possessions should be seen as common property "in the sense that they should accrue to the benefit not only of themselves but of others." The clarity and force of the teaching can be seen in two further statements: "The right to have a share of earthly goods sufficient for oneself and one's family belongs to everyone. . . . If someone is in extreme necessity, such a one has the right to take from the riches of others what he or she needs."[18]

The momentum of Vatican II was not lost on Paul VI, at least at the beginning of his pontificate, which coincided with the last

62 A NEW IDEOLOGY:

two years of Vatican II. He issued two highly important documents, *Populorum Progressio* and *Octogesima Adveniens*.

In 1967, a year before the Medellín conference, *Populorum
Progressio* rejected many of the basic precepts of capitalism, including unrestricted private property, the unbridled profit mo-
tive, and reliance on free trade in the international economy. Paul
VI emphasizes very strongly the right, in justice, of poorer nations to aid by wealthier nations. There is at least a suggestion
that, in extreme situations, the poor are justified in a violent solution to their problems. That statement or interpretation was modified by Paul on his arrival at Medellín.

He describes the modern world: the rich are getting richer, and
the poor, poorer—an analysis even more valid in the 1980s than it
was in 1967. It was also the type of analysis that would be echoed
at Medellín. Paul looks beyond poverty to its causes: systems of
modern economics are widening the gap between rich and poor.
And this gap is perceived by the poor. Why? Because the spread
of modern communications has brought with it a revolution of
rising expectations. "One cannot condemn such abuses [of liberal
capitalism] too strongly because the economy should be at the
service of humankind."[19]

Octogesima Adveniens, an apostolic letter issued in 1971 on the
eightieth anniversary of *Rerum Novarum*, covers a number of
topics. Among the more important themes treated is socialism.
Paul again distinguishes between movements (or regimes) and the
original ideology of socialism. Socialism is no longer rejected.
Instead careful judgment is called for. And socialism must safe-
guard such values as freedom, responsibility, and openness to the
spiritual dimension of the human person.

A review of the social teachings of the church shows a number
of changes and advances. The church begins to employ a new
methodology. The perspective has changed: no longer is it church
and world, or the church in the world, but rather the church for
the world. This is a major shift. Advances in social teaching place
the church at the side of the poor, helping them claim what is
theirs. The church also shifts its focus from alleviation of the results of poverty to elimination of the causes of poverty. The
church increases its questioning of liberal capitalism and makes a
cautious opening to socialism. It is important to keep these

changes in mind when attempting to understand the venture undertaken by Latin American liberation theologians.

Methodology

Liberation theology offers Latin America religious leadership groups a new way to do theology. Indeed, some critics have said that the theology of liberation is nothing but methodology and lacks ascertainable content. That criticism is heard less and less as Latin American theologians add more and more flesh to the skeletal beginning made by Gutiérrez and other pioneers.

Liberation theologians have made strong claims that their methodology is new, distinct from traditional theology. This claim is made, in part, to give character, weight, and distinctness to their thought. Whether, in fact, their theological method is new can be debated.

The lines of influence in the creation of the methodology of liberation theology have yet to be untangled by historians. At this time it is enough to say that the conciliar fathers in *Gaudium et Spes*, the architects of Medellín and Puebla, and the liberation theologians themselves consistently follow the same three-step methodology.

The first step is a description of the church in the world. This step involves the use of sociology and economics. And in the case of the Latin Americans at least (in contrast to some originators of feminist or black theology in the U.S.A.), their analysis is structural analysis, deriving in part from class and dependency analysis, a point that will be developed more fully later in this chapter.

Then as a second step comes biblical and doctrinal reflection on the situation described. Thus in the case of Latin America, the teaching of the Bible and of the church led the bishops at Medellín and Puebla and the theologians of liberation to reflect on a society in which justice would prevail. This they describe as a society in which human dignity is respected, the legitimate aspirations of the people are satisfied, personal freedom and access to truth are guaranteed. This type of society, which would correspond to Christian principles, conflicts with what the bishops and theologians perceive in Latin America: they find oppression by power groups, elites. "[These] groups may give the impression of maintaining peace and order, but in truth it is nothing but the continuous and inevitable seed of rebellion and war."[20]

As a third stage, pastoral conclusions follow the biblical and doctrinal reflections. Some conclusions that have consistently appeared in CELAM documents and in the writings of theologians of liberation include defense of the rights of the oppressed, a healthy critical sense of the social situation, promotion of grassroots organizations, a halt to the arms race in Latin America and in the world, just prices for raw materials, and a denunciation of the machinations of world powers that work against the self-determination of weaker powers.

Gutiérrez and other liberation theologians contrast their theology with traditional (largely deductive) theology. They emphasize that their theology is a second act or step, not a first act, as is traditional theology. Liberation theology is elaborated in making reflections on reality; it develops out of praxis.[21] This praxis is the core of understanding how liberation theologians conceive their methodology.

Praxis for them is a somewhat vague term with unfixed parameters. At times it refers to the activity of hierarchy, clergy, and other church professionals. At other times it has been made to designate actions of the entire ecclesial community in conformity with the message of the gospel; this is usually referred to as "orthopraxis." Sometimes praxis refers to the conduct of the individual believer within an essentially social dimension.

Praxis is used in a larger sense than it has had from the days of the Greek philosophers, and especially larger than its Marxian usage. Praxis is a way of knowing. It means learning by reflecting on experience. This is exactly how Gutiérrez defines theology: critical reflection on the activity of the church.

It is important to note that this is not a detached reflection by an analyst pouring over facts gathered by academics. The first moment or act for Gutiérrez is charity—doing justice in action; then theology can be practiced as a second act. Juan Luis Segundo is even stronger in drawing out the practical inferences for the doing of this new theology: it cannot be learned, as traditional theology was, behind seminary walls by teachers and students isolated from the day-by-day struggles of the church in the world, meaning especially the poor in the world.

Hence not only does theology have a new meaning; "church" does also. Traditional theology, until Vatican II, had emphasized the church as believers organized in a hierarchical, institutional body. Liberation theology uses both class analysis and biblical analysis. Thus it sees the church and the world in terms of class; within the social classes the poor are the most favored by God. This option for the poor is for liberation theologians a biblical imperative.

The first act or moment of the liberation theologian is action on the part of the poor, on the side of the poor, in the senses of identification, geography, and advocacy. This understanding of theology seems very far from its usual meaning in North America and Europe. In practice liberation theology may not be that distinct, but liberation theologians have found it helpful to define themselves clearly and often in contrast to traditional theology.

The understanding of praxis thus is more specific in liberation theology than a John Dewey philosophy of learning from experience. Liberation theology means learning from the experience of the poor.

Theology of Liberation and Traditional Theology

Until the Vatican II era traditional theology formed the basis for the education of the Latin American clergy and laity. Neoscholasticism ruled the Catholic theological world ever since the sixteenth century. It had its supremacy reinforced by Leo XIII at the end of the nineteenth century, when he issued his letter *Aeterni Patris* reestablishing Scholasticism as the philosophical and theological system for the church and mandating Thomistic Scholasticism for seminary education.

Theologians and philosophers outside and inside the Catholic Church acknowledge the greatness of Thomas Aquinas's intellectual system. For years followers of the Great Book Program read major sections of Thomas's *Summa Theologiae*. That work is regarded as the greatest of medieval theology. Without a knowledge of the *Summa* or a similar monument of Scholastic thought, one would be hard put to understand either medieval or Reformation thought. However, enshrining one school of thought as *the* intellectual system of the church was a profound mistake.

Liberation thought was not the first to point out the deficiencies of Scholasticism, but liberation theology has become one of the most effective theological expressions done in conscious contrast to traditional theology. How far the apple fell from the tree is a valid question: despite the protestations of Oliveros and others that the theology of liberation is new and distinct, liberation theology deeply roots itself in neo-scholasticism.

Traditional theology and liberation theology mirror many of the cleavages in the old and new Latin American church. Several characteristics mark Scholasticism as distinct from liberation (and many other types of modern) theology: Scholasticism is "eternal," ahistorical, essentialist (as opposed to existentialist), theocentric, hierarchical, and feudal. By contrast liberation theologians characterize their thought as evolutionary, historical, existentialist, christocentric, communitarian, participatory, and egalitarian.

Many divergences of thought in the Latin American church center around the person of French philosopher Jacques Maritain. A neo-scholastic, he influenced several generations of Latin American intellectuals and Catholic Actionists. Latin Americans read him in French or in translations of his numerous works. And he indirectly affected Latin Americans through teachers and writers such as Fernando Martínez Paz of Argentina and Tristão de Athayde (Alceu Amoroso Lima) of Brazil.

Maritain captures well the spirit of traditional Catholic thought. Writing about Aristotle's thought, the basis of Scholasticism, Maritain stated:

> To extract the truth latent in Platonism was the mighty reform effected by Aristotle. Aristotle successfully took to pieces Plato's system, adapted to the exigencies of reality the formal principles he had discovered and misapplied, reducing his sweeping perspectives within limits imposed by a sublime common sense, and thus saved everything vital in his master's thought. He did more: he founded for all time the true philosophy. If he saved whatever was true and valuable, not only in Plato, but in all the ancient thinkers of Greece, and brought to successful conclusion the great work

of synthesis which Plato had attempted, it was because he definitively secured the attainment of reality by the human intellect. His work was not only the natural fruit of Greek wisdom purified from Plato's mistakes and the alien elements included in Platonism; it contained, completely formed and potentially capable of unlimited growth, the body of the universal human philosophy.

Then [Thomas Aquinas] welded Aristotelian thought into a powerful and harmonious system; he explored its principles, cleared its conclusions, enlarged its horizons; and, if he rejected nothing, he added much, enriching it with the immense wealth of Latin Christian tradition, restoring in their proper places many of Plato's doctrines, on certain fundamental points opening up entirely new perspectives, and thus giving proof of a philosophic genius as mighty as Aristotle himself. Finally, and this was his supreme achievement, when by his genius as a theologian he made use of Aristotle's philosophy as the instrument of the sacred science, he raised philosophy above itself by submitting it to the illumination of a higher light, which invested its truth with a radiance more divine than human.[22]

In brief, Maritain and neo-scholastics in general believed that Aristotle and Aquinas gave the church an intellectual system that was established in its essentials and needed only to be understood and expanded, mostly in nonessential aspects.

Maritain represents a frame of mind that has disappeared from most Catholic seminaries and universities in Latin America. But that traditional caste of mind continues a vestigial existence in right-wing Catholics of Brazil, Argentina, Chile and Central America who joined *Tradición, Familia, y Patria* (Tradition, Family, and Fatherland). And it continues among military men who formed or passed on the doctrine of national security. Brazilian and Argentinian presidents and military commanders regularly make appeals for order and stability on the basis of Catholic integralism (Western Christian civilization vaguely undergirded by Scholasticism).

Changes in Latin American theology and practice are profoundly rooted in advances that were taking place in European

Catholic thought. These changes multiplied and created new expressions of Catholic theology especially during the 1950s and '60s. The theology behind Vatican II was taking shape in Catholic universities and departments of theology at state universities in France, Germany, Holland, and Belgium. At precisely this period Latin American bishops and religious superiors sent off some of their brightest talent to European schools for theological training. A significant convergence was taking place of the Latin American church and new European thought.

Gustavo Gutiérrez, who would become a central figure in liberation theology, enrolled as a student in philosophy at Louvain and then in the school of theology at Lyons. Both institutions helped lead the church toward new (or revived) forms of philosophical and theological expression. Gutiérrez experienced at first hand what leading intellectuals of the Catholic Church were going through: the shift from neo-scholasticism to contemporary European theology with a variety of approaches.

What Gutiérrez heard or read at Louvain and Lyons was the fruit of many years of effort on the part of Catholic and Protestant intellectuals in Europe. For a long time their efforts had been marked by a return to sources: Catholics and Protestants alike searched the scriptures and the writings of the fathers of the church. These biblical and patristic endeavors developed into full-scale movements. The Ecole Biblique was founded in Jerusalem before World War I; the Institutum Biblicum opened in Rome. Numerous archeological explorations began. Interest in biblical languages revived and journals devoted to biblical and patristic studies multiplied.

A parallel exploration into modern philosophy began. A number of Catholic and Protestant intellectuals searched for philosophical approaches that could be Christian without being Scholastic. They favored an approach that was historical, acknowledging Aristotle and Aquinias as important figures in the history of Western thought but not putting them dead center as did Maritain.

At Louvain Gutiérrez encountered a school of neo-Thomism cautiously exploring contemporary philosophy. Students heard moderate and historically-minded neo-scholastics. And they were introduced to phenomenology and other forms of modern philosophy. It was an era of exploration. Creativity and search were even more evident at the Louvain theological center. A number of thinkers who influenced the progress of contemporary theology taught at Louvain: Bede Rigaux, O.F.M., in biblical exegesis, Roger Aubert in church history, Philippe Delhaye in ecclesiology, and above all Gustave Thils in theological methodology.

The faculty at Lyons matched the intellectual stimulation of Louvain and presented Gutiérrez with additional perspectives from modern theology. Theologians there suffered some of the frustrations following in the wake of *Humanae Generis*, an attempt by Rome to dampen efforts at nonscholastic theologizing. But Roman efforts did not weaken for long the vitality of such journals as *Nouvelle Théologie*, emanating from the Jesuit faculty at Lyons. Pioneers of modern Catholic theology at Lyons, such as Henri de Lubac, continued their search for new biblical knowledge and their study of modern philosophy.

That liberation theology is profoundly rooted in European theological experience can be seen in Gutiérrez's *A Theology of Liberation*. Several hundred references are made to works of Yves Congar, Gustave Thils, Karl Rahner, and a whole panoply of European intellectuals—theologians and philosophers alike. It would be a cruel joke for Latin American theologians of liberation not to acknowledge their European heritage.

Besides differences in the perspectives already described, liberation and traditional theology differ in their starting points. Traditional theologians begin by examining scriptural or traditional Christian teaching. For liberation theologians the starting point is the poor—more concretely stated, the experience of the poor in a history that is at the same time religious and secular, individual and collective, embracing the worlds of consciousness and external forces. This theme will be elaborated in a later section.

The tools that liberation theologians use to examine and understand experience—the experience of the poor and the efforts of the church in their behalf—do not come primarily from philosophy but from the social sciences. Here then is another difference between traditional theology and liberation theology. There is a good deal less emphasis on philosophy in liberation thought. Instead social science becomes its chief auxiliary in theological analysis.

One would be misled to understand "social science" here to

mean primarily social and economic statistics or sociological and economic theories as they typically are taught in the classrooms of American universities.[23] Beyond the facts of the Latin American situation are sociological constructs that liberation theologians feel are crucial in explaining how Latin America is currently evolving. In the main, there are two such constructs: class analysis and dependency theory. The theologians began by stating facts of Latin American underdevelopment: there are great numbers of poor persons and "nonpersons" (persons who do not participate fully or at all in the benefits of the system) and, relatively speaking, the poor are becoming poorer. Then the theologians (often pressed by other Latin American intellectuals) needed to explain why the situation is what it is.

For this explanation they engaged in discussion with their colleagues in the social sciences. Of course, there is more than one explanation taught in Latin America. (One may hear Ricardo Ffrench-Davis explain the Latin American economic picture in terms similar to those of Milton Friedman, from whom Ffrench-Davis learned his economics.) But the prevailing view in sociology and economics in Latin America leans toward class analysis and dependency theory.

Class analysis and dependency theory go hand in hand. As already mentioned, the failure of development models to benefit the Latin American masses brought dependency theory to the forefront in Latin American intellectual circles. Dependency theory sees development and underdevelopment as necessarily connected: they are complementary parts of the unity of the capitalist system. Underdeveloped countries—countries on the periphery of the global economic system—are deluded if they think they have the possibility of development within the existing capitalist system. These countries will always remain dependent on the developed countries. Besides the iron laws of the international marketplace, which tip the balance in favor of the developed countries, especially the U.S.A., other mechanisms of control are the multinational corporations and the international banking community. The latter includes both public entities, such as the International Monetary Fund, and private interests, such as Chase Manhattan, Citibank, and the Bank America.

Class analysis explains that this dominance is made possible through the cooperation of small groups of local citizens—elitist oligarchies. Both new (industrial) and old (farming and ranching) oligarchies are intimately tied in with the world capitalist system and help it run. An oligarchy holds national political power or controls it sufficiently to conform to its interests. Often the interests of the military and the national oligarchy coincide. (The one exception was Peru where dependency analysis led the military to believe that the existence of the landholding oligarchy created an incendiary situation that threatened national security from within the country.)

In the view of class analysis the oligarchies form an almost seamless international upper and upper-middle social class. They adopt cultural characteristics of the developed nations and disdain their own indigenous cultures. Whether seen on Lexington or Collins avenues or in Miraflores, Las Lomas de San Isidro, or Chapinero, they all have the same look about them.

The fact that this analysis derives from Karl Marx and his followers does not deter liberation theologians. They accept these explanations as factual or at least as better explanations of reality than those provided by structural functionalism in American sociology or Keynesian economics. For many Latin Americans, such theories are bankrupt.

Nonetheless for many North Americans the fact that liberation analysis is neo-Marxist is a serious matter.[24] In response Latin American moderates have pointed out several factors that caution against overhasty condemnation. First, one may borrow parts of Marxist analysis without being a Marxist, much less a communist. Secondly, Marx is recognized by even non-Marxist sociologists as a great sociologist. He called attention to social class as a factor in social life in a way that no other sociologist had done. In this and other regards, Marx is one of the pioneers of theoretical and empirical sociology. Thirdly, American sociologists and social journalists have done innumerable studies based on class. In fact, class analysis of a particular kind is regarded as a kind of illness many American sociologists suffer from, a kind of adolescent fixation that inhibits consideration of other factors, such as ethnicity. Fourthly, one is invited by Latin Americans to see whether class analysis and dependency theory do not in fact explain a great deal.

By the same token dependency explanations of the Latin American situation and *dependencia* as a general theory have serious limitations and weaknesses.[25] As a theory, *dependencia* does not explain many of the social and economic processes in the history of Latin America, as many social scientists and historians have pointed out.[26] Moreover—and for some this is the most important critique—*dependencia* analysts have failed to formulate alternative strategies for social change.[27] In sum, as John Browett remarks, the dependency perspective "provides some understanding of the basic causes of the contradictions within capitalism but does little to generate proposals for their elimination."[28]

Meanwhile many liberation theologians continue to use—uncritically—dependency perspectives in reflecting on the Latin American situation. Although many of their social science colleagues have attempted to move beyond *dependencia* as an all-encompassing theory, liberation theologians prefer to moralize about *dependencia* as the central "reality" of Latin America.[29]

A final difference between liberation theology and traditional theology is the choice of audience to which it is addressed. Traditional theology addresses itself to other theologians or to students of theology. This is nowhere more evident than in Thomas Aquinas. His *Summa Theologiae* begins with questions from other notable theologians or his own students; his main argumentations and responses to questions are addressed to the same audience. Most academic theology is done in the same manner. When Norman Pittinger, who has published fifty theological works, was asked who was the interlocutor he had in mind when he wrote his books, he replied it was other theologians. Did he have the poor in mind? "No."[30]

Liberation theologians have the poor in mind when they do their theology. More precisely they have the nonperson in mind. By this they mean what they call the "marginalized," those pushed to the margins of society by culturally embedded discrimination. These are the "invisible" persons who have been treated until recently as if they did not exist: women, blacks, the urban and rural poor.

To its credit, modern European theology has attempted to shift its focus from other theologians to nonbelievers. Historians of contemporary theology point out that European theologians, such as Rahner and Congar, who dominated the thinking of Vatican II, attempted to modernize church thinking. But for them treating the church in the modern world meant addressing the questions of science and the difficulties of belief in the post-Enlightenment world.

To Latin American theologians such questions are perhaps interesting, but they are not primarily their questions. It is not the nonbeliever but rather the nonperson who is the subject to be addressed. Such is the extent of this difference that Latin American theologians were shocked by the "callousness" of Harvey Cox's speculation in *The Secular City* about life in an ultratechnical society, as Oliveros reports.[31]

Latin American theologians believe that theology should be a response to the questions of the people. As Robert McAfee Brown comments, today it is the poor, the "nonpersons," who are asking the questions.[32] Basic questions in theology are approached very differently as a result of differing perspectives. Classic theologians ask about proofs for the existence of God in an age of science. Liberation theologians ask, Does that God interest us?

As Juan Luis Segundo mentions, there is a long tradition of spending a great deal of time on the "first questions" (the existence and nature of God).[33] It was not unknown in schools of theology for professors to spend a whole semester on the first two questions of the *Summa*. Such a preoccupation is deplored by many Latin Americans, one of whom is quoted by Segundo as saying that he wishes he could punch around St. Irenaeus and others who wasted so much time debating questions about the "substantial nature" of God.

In contrast to traditional theology, Segundo points out that there is a fact of life that appears more decisive: "among Christians [in Latin America] we find a real lack of interest in the problem of God. If Vatican II had said that there were three Gods, who would care?" He asks, What does God say about himself in the New Testament? God's "statements for the most part deal with us human beings, our lives, and how to transform them. A much smaller set of statements deal with God. But even these passages show [God] operating in our lives and transforming our history." Thus Segundo hints that "God appears on the human horizon in the process of transforming [human] existence from within." He goes on to argue the radical proposition that "our God is fashioned partly in the image of the social reality of Christian Western society."[34]

This is not the place to develop further such ideas. It is more important to note the difference in approach and style that arises from the difference in audiences that traditional and liberation theologians have in mind. Traditional theology, addressing the educated Christian on the verge of unbelief or the upper middle-class unbeliever, begins with questions about the existence of God. Liberation theology, having in mind the questions of the poor and marginalized, asks about idolatry: do Christians by their lives present false images of God to others?[35] In this analysis, liberation theologians are developing their thought along the lines of *Gaudium et Spes*, which states: "To the extent that they are deficient in their religious, moral, or social life, Christians must be said to conceal rather than reveal the authentic face of God and religion."[36]

Theologians of Liberation

History will record few single names as giants in liberation theology as one might point to Thomas Aquinas in Scholasticism or Martin Luther in Reformation thought. A number of intellectuals have taken up the work of liberation thought; they have contributed but a part to the larger enterprise. Although theology of liberation was not invented by a committee, it has been the result of cooperative endeavor to an extent previously unknown in Western philosophy or theology.

Because of the cooperation needed and the ad hoc nature of the liberation theology undertaking, communication among the system-builders assumes central importance. Theologians and their colleagues in the biblical and social sciences exchange information, analyses, and definitions through letters, conferences, and publications. One finds contributions to liberation thought in mimeographed position papers as well as published books.

Paulo Freire and Gustavo Gutiérrez have been preeminent in the creation of liberation thought. Their contributions have allowed liberation theology to move along paths it might not have taken without them. Whatever may be the ultimate judgment on the worth of their efforts, they are to date the most representative of liberation thinkers and will be treated at greater length below. If someone is looking for "classics" to read in liberation thought, Freire's *Pedagogy of the Oppressed* and Gutiérrez's *A Theology of Liberation* cannot be ignored.

Paulo Freire: Conscientization

Not only is the method of creating theology or ideology different in Latin American theology; the method of communicating this ideology is also different. At the core of what many Latin Americans mean when they talk about education as a liberating force is not so much the thought of Gustavo Gutiérrez as that of Paulo Freire.

Freire is better known worldwide than is Gutiérrez. This is due in part to the position Freire occupied at the World Council of Churches, headquartered in Geneva. This position offered him an international platform from which to radiate his influence. Freire's work is widely perceived as a philosophy of education, so his thought appeals to wider audiences—audiences that are less churchy, if not altogether secular. He has been invited on two occasions to lecture for a quarter at the Harvard School of Education. His best-known book, *The Pedagogy of the Oppressed*, was available at most university bookstores in the United States. It is a book that is used both as text and reference, despite the heavy-going character of its prose and style.[37]

Unlike Gutiérrez and many of the liberation theologians, Freire did not study in European universities. Nonetheless he was influenced strongly by European and North American writers such as Husserl, Buber, Mounier, Schaff, and Fromm. He also immersed himself in the lives of the poverty-stricken masses of northeast Brazil. Out of both sources, Freire developed a coherent intellectual system and a practical methodology.

As a professor at the University of Recife, his area of interest was history and philosophy of education. What he was searching for was a philosophy and a practical program for training adults to read and write. Together with a number of other young Catholic intellectuals, he joined Catholic Action, thereby becoming involved in adult education.

Freire, though, was interested in far more than functional liter-

acy. He wanted to empower illiterates, to raise their consciousness of their own fatalism—to conscientize them—and to motivate them to take charge of their lives to a greater extent. It was no
wonder then that the literacy movement was considered revolutionary or that the Brazilian military, when it came to power in
1964, dismantled the movement.

Freire suffered an experience that was to become increasingly
common for Catholic intellectuals. He was jailed for two months.
He then left for Chile rather than face a series of "preventive"
arrests. There he continued his work, this time under U.N. aus-
pices as educational consultant for INRA, an agrarian reform
program.

The force of Freire's ideas and methods can be felt in reading
his *Pedagogy of the Oppressed*. Some North Americans feel that
his ideas challenge the status quo so strongly and so inevitably
that it is better not to conscientize the poor and illiterate. Of forty
education majors interviewed at a large state university in the
U.S.A., all admired Freire's method but the majority thought the
method should not be employed, because of possible social consequences.[38] In effect, better not to tell the poor the truth about
themselves.

Freire, of course, would disagree. So would the theologians of
liberation. It is only a slight exaggeration to say that their whole
effort has been to tell the poor (and the nonpoor) the truth about
poverty and disenfranchisement. Freire and the other liberation
thinkers also argue against *not* educating oppressors and oppressed. The liberation argument is that education is never neu-
tral. Left to itself, conventional education socializes students into
the values and worldview of oppressors.

Like other Brazilians in the early 1960s, Freire worked out for
himself an intellectual position about underdevelopment and
backwardness. He saw a new era dawning for Brazil, one in which
economically there would be greater national development and
autonomy, and socio-politically there would be more openness
and participation. The process of modernization would tend to
divide society into one group that would resist change through
paternalism and "massification" and another group that would
welcome necessary changes. Freire felt that he and other educa-
tors must fit into the second category: they must help to prepare
themselves and others for modernization.

Freire viewed traditional literacy training as a mechanism for adjusting the illiterate to a given society. Its methods treated disadvantaged human beings as objects into which superior beings poured knowledge. For Freire this is debasing and dehumanizing. The human person, for him, is not an object but a "subject," one who works upon and changes the world.

Freire proposed a critical, active method that would overcome fatalism and resignation. The critical capacity of the illiterate grows out of discussions about situations that "mean something" to them, and to which they themselves have something to contribute. The teacher serves as facilitator and catalyst for this dialogue.

Freire and his associates developed a core vocabulary out of the de facto life situations of the rural poor. This varied from region to region so that words and concepts used in programs in Brazil differed from some of those used in Chile. There are stages in the Freire method, but we cannot describe them here in detail. What is important and what has been seized upon in other parts of the world—and by pioneeers in other types of liberation theology, such as black or feminist liberation theology—is that it is necessary for repressed groupings of persons to reflect on their own cultural, economic, and social situation and to begin to become masters of their own lives. *Conscientization* won a place for itself at the heart of liberation thought.

Gustavo Gutiérrez: Theology of Liberation

Roger Vekemans, in his three-part study of the history of the theology of liberation, examines a number of "antecedents."[39] His discussion is probably more confusing than helpful. Vekemans' study makes it appear that the theology of liberation developed out of other currents of thought in some straightline fashion. But Gustavo Gutiérrez and other major architects of the theology of liberation are at pains to point out that they did not pertain to this or that antecedent school of thought.

Nonetheless, theology of liberation has its intellectual debts, some of which are traceable to currents of thought of the 1960s and '70s. Mention of the antecedents of liberation thought helps to picture the color and texture of the intellectual landscape in which the theology of liberation was created. The major currents and themes of those times as they affected Latin America included the theology of revolution, the theology of development, dialogue with Marxists, the theology of hope, and political theology. Most of these themes were more European or North American in terms of major participants, interlocutors, and methodologies. The theology of revolution seemed almost to be a direct funneling of ideas of Richard Shaull of Princeton Theological Seminary and the National Council of Churches to Montevideo and thereafter to other parts of Latin America through ISAL. Most of the intellectual development of the theology of revolution took place in Europe.

In part, it was the extraterritorial nature of these discussions that sparked the beginning of the theology of liberation. Under the urgency of preparation for the forthcoming Medellín conference, Latin American theologians turned to the theme of latinamericanization. The uniqueness of Latin American theology is the burden of this chapter.

The breakthrough occurred when Gustavo Gutiérrez presented a major statement of Latin American thought at the Chimbote conference in July 1968, immediately preceding the Medellín conference. The nucleus of his presentation (published under the title *Hacia una teología de la liberación* the following year) was that it was not development that Latin America needed but liberation.[40] He saw development as an idea that was promoted by non-Latin Americans, was clearly bankrupt in Latin America, and was not the response called for after meditating on the Latin American situation in the light of sacred scripture and tradition, especially the social justice tradition of the church.

It is sometimes believed that the theology of liberation developed out of the Medellín conference.[41] A first rough sketch of the theology of liberation was presented at the Chimbote conference, before Medellín, but the formulation of liberation theology began in 1964, when Ivan Illich, then a major catalyst of Latin American thought, organized the meeting in Petrópolis mentioned above. By all accounts Gutiérrez's contribution to that meeting was the most significant theologically. In a paper on the pastoral ministry of the church, Gutiérrez developed the theme of theology as critical reflection on praxis.[42] He further reworked and presented that theme for a group of Catholic university movement leaders in Montevideo in February 1967.[43] These were the first stages in the elaboration of Gutiérrez's thought.

Another stage came in the mid-1960s when political activists, including a number of convinced Christians, began to take up arms against corrupt governments. The new political awareness, already described, and the "new" definition of the Latin American situation posed by these activists troubled Gutiérrez. They forced him to come to terms with problems that his theology, largely learned in many years of study in Europe, was incapable of even addressing, much less solving.

A further stage in the development of Gutiérrez's formulations can be dated to July 1967. At that time he gave a course on poverty in Montreal. He viewed the poor from a new perspective: they were both a social class and the bearers of God's word.

After presentation of the rough sketch of liberation thought at Chimbote, he continued the elaboration of his thought at an international conference in Cartigny, Switzerland, sponsored by Sodepax. By now Gutiérrez was gaining international attention. His paper for the conference was published in several languages;[44] an English resumé was issued as *Notes on a Theology of Liberation*.[45]

During the ensuing months Gutiérrez worked diligently on a more elaborate and polished version of his thought. The result was *A Theology of Liberation*. It appeared in 1971 in Spanish and thereafter was translated into many other languages. It is acknowledged as a classic presentation of the theology of liberation. There are many theologies of liberation and many variations within mainline liberation thought, but Gutiérrez's work remains the most representative and the best known.

When lecturing in the United States, which he has done with some frequency, including a semester at Union Theological Seminary, he apologizes that the language he will be speaking is neither English nor Spanish but his own special blend. When speaking of the death of the theologian, a possibility that must be faced by those who take a stand against a violent, entrenched status quo, his fingers play nervously over his face.

By South American standards, Gutiérrez is a "late vocation." Instead of entering the seminary after six years of primary school or even after high school, he entered the school of medicine at the

Universidad Nacional San Marcos in Lima. Like many of his
classmates, he was active in political groups. Always interested in
issues beyond medicine, after five years of medicine he shifted to
philosophical and theological studies to prepare for the priesthood. He studied for a semester in Santiago, which offered the
best in theological education in Latin America at the time. That
best was none too strong, though, and Gutiérrez moved to
Europe. First, beginning in 1951, he studied philosophy and psychology at the Catholic University of Louvain. Then, in 1955, he
went to Lyons to study theology. He was ordained in Lima in
1959, and returned to Europe for one semester at the Jesuit Gre-
gorian University in Rome.

Aside from lecture tours to various parts of the world, Gutiérrez has remained in Lima since 1960. There he has been professor
of theology at the Catholic University and national advisor for
the National Union of Catholic Students. Currently he prefers
not to be known as a *profesor universitario*; instead, in responding to the question about what he is doing in Lima, he answers
that "I work with the people," and he does theology out of that
context.[46]

Other Theologians of Liberation

Many of the other creators of the theology of liberation have
had educational experiences similar to those of Gutiérrez.
Leonardo Boff, who is best known for his development of liberation christology, pursued higher studies in Europe after doing his
basic philosophical and theological studies in Brazil. Boff concentrated his graduate studies in Munich, where he studied with
leading contemporary theologians—Rahner, Scheffczyk, and
Fries—but he also sat in on courses at Louvain, Würzburg, and
Oxford.

Hugo Assmann also went to Europe after basic philosophical
and theological studies in Brazil. He went to Rome for graduate
theology but then studied the social sciences and mass communications at various Latin American universities. The multidisci-
plinary training of Assmann and many other theologians of
liberation is nowhere better exemplified than in the training of
Enrique Dussel, one of the few lay liberation theologians (mar-

ried, the father of three children). He received a licentiate in philosophy from the Universidad de Cuyó in Mendoza, Argentina, and a doctorate in philosophy from the Universidad Nacional de Madrid. Then he studied for two degrees in Paris: a doctorate in history from the Sorbonne and a licentiate in theology from the Institut Catholique.

Dussel also exemplifies two other characteristics found in a number of other proponents of the theology of liberation: he is in exile and he has been brushed by death. His home in Argentina was bombed. Perhaps this helps to explain Gutiérrez's anxious fingers.

Another pioneer of liberation theology, especially at the level of popularization, is Juan Luis Segundo. He studied philosophy in Argentina, then attended Louvain for a licentiate in theology and moved to the University of Paris for a doctorate in letters. Interestingly, for the latter degree he wrote works on the thought of Nicolas Berdyaev and on ecclesiology.

Some Protestant proponents of liberation theology received their higher theological education in the United States. José Míguez Bonino attended Emory University and Union Theological Seminary; Rubem Alves went to Princeton University and Union Theological Seminary. Both have also been visiting professors in the United States.

Several common characteristics can be noted about some of the leading liberation theologians. They are serious students who have been exposed at length to ideas outside Latin America. Their intellectual training usually involved more than one discipline. They are committed to the liberation struggle and, in many instances, have suffered personally and deeply. Finally they have attempted to construct an indigenous Latin American theology. How well they have done so we shall have reason to judge as we move to a direct consideration of their thought.

Fundamental Themes

Liberation theology is nothing like a finished system of thought. It was continually criticized, especially in the early and mid-1970s, for having little or no content. Where was a christology or an ecclesiology in liberation theology? Where was the trini-

tarian doctrine? How about spirituality? Much of this criticism
was correct but undeserved. Liberation theologians were well
aware of their paucity of thought in major areas of traditional
theological concerns. The most palatable and promising response
they could give was: it is coming. Liberation theologians knew
this in their bones and did not always bother to explain other
reasons.

For one thing, they were not necessarily concerned with the
same questions as were followers of traditional theology. (It
would take wild broncos to pull them into a traditional consideration of the Trinity. They are, however, vitally concerned with the
life of God.) Secondly, they believed it impertinent at best and
haughty and insensitive at worst for European and North American critics to expect a fully developed theological system "overnight." Outsiders tend to forget that liberation theology is not the
work of a Paul Tillich who could produce a fully developed system within ten to twenty years. Rather, liberation theology is the
product of a number of theologians working in different locations and without a principal figure directing them. Thirdly, liberation theology is developing out of immersion with the people,
"at the base," and this takes time. But it also allows for development, revision, and honing of thought. It is clearly an evolutionary process.

At first certain central themes emerged in the work of Latin
American theologians living in far-distant locations. Latin
Americans sometimes took this communality and centrality of
themes chosen by diverse individuals and groups working sepa-
rately to be evidence of "the working of the Spirit." But the fact
of this common emergence should not be surprising: many persons were reflecting on similar situations throughout Latin
America (and the Third World) and they were using a process
modeled for all at Vatican II. Moreover, countless meetings,
seminars, courses, and conferences on liberation themes were
taking place in Latin America as early as 1962. Many meetings
took place because of the intrinsic dynamism of liberation
thought and the necessity of further enriching partially developed
insights.

Another, more regular channel of communication was developed in these two decades beyond occasional meetings. Theologi-

cal and pastoral thought was communicated in numerous publications: newsletters, pamphlets, and magazines. Their number was immense. Every group seemed to have its own internal bulletin, many of them developing or diffusing liberation thought. Some liberation theology is still being developed in mimeographed bulletins with a circulation of a hundred or less but most major advances now appear as articles in *Christus,* the *Revista Eclesiástica Brasileira*, or a number of other journals.[47]

Out of this interaction has grown a network of theologians and another network of readers. The theologians of liberation know one another personally, despite the distances between their home bases of activity, and they are aware of one another's latest thoughts. Thus about one hundred liberation theologians communicate with one another informally but regularly through conferences, letters, and published works. Another group of consumers (many of them out of Latin America) tries to keep up with liberation thought through personal contact or through major theological journals from Latin America.

Discussing the theology of liberation is like hearing the report on a friend's teenage son or daughter: the report tends to confuse outsiders because of growth in some areas and not in others, because of extremes in stances and moods, and because of enthusiasms for some areas of thought and unexplained dislike for other areas. In liberation theology all this takes place with a resolute distancing from previous schools of theology, especially those of the First World, while at the same time implicitly depending on the insights of modern European and North American theology.

Description of Reality

Although the three methodological divisions—description of the Latin American situation, theological reflection, and pastoral applications—seldom appear neatly in the writings of the theologians of liberation, the divisions are clearly agreed to as the major steps in doing liberation theology. This became abundantly clear in the large-scale theological conference on theological method that took place in Mexico City in 1975.[48]

For most theologians of liberation the task of describing Latin

American society was sufficiently well accomplished by the Medellín and Puebla conferences. They might prefer a stronger touch here or there but by and large they take such analysis for granted and are now developing other "parts" (they prefer "moments" or "movements") of liberation theology.

The description of Latin American society was done largely by using dependency and class analysis. Theologians who contributed to this analysis include Gutiérrez, Dussel, Assmann, Rubem Alves, Sergio Méndez Arceo, and Raúl Vidales. They concentrate on themes such as the prevalence and condition of nonpersons in Latin America, the existence of social sin (structural or institutionalized injustice), the spiral of violence (Hélder Câmara's phrase), and the injustices of world capitalism. These themes have been discussed in the previous chapter.

Unity of History

The major debt of liberation theologians to modern European theology is the acceptance of the unity of history. To non-Catholics and especially to non-Christians this may not appear as a major achievement but for Latin Americans it is a crucial shift in thinking, in fact a quantum leap. Instead of thinking of religious history and world history as separate, instead of believing that outside the church there is no salvation, instead of talking about religious or secular activity, liberation theologians routinely and strongly emphasize the unity of history.

Medieval and Reformation theology emphasized the distinction of natural and supernatural worlds, separate worlds of secular and divine activity, worlds that did not always have much to do with one another. In the extreme, in the theology of Martin Luther, there were two kingdoms; activity in the secular kingdom could not affect life in the other kingdom, the world of grace and God's activity.

This distinction was denied by the Second Vatican Council and the consequent affirmation of the unity of history has become the major rationale for the involvement of the Latin American church in the social and political world. The shift in perspective from an other-worldly to a this-worldly ideology is extreme.

The question of the unity of history has been worked out in

terms of nature and grace. This has been a major task of modern Catholic theology, especially as developed in the works of Rahner and de Lubac and expressed in *Gaudium et Spes* at Vatican II. Nature and grace are no longer seen as separable areas of human existence but rather two dimensions of one "graced nature." As Míguez Bonino has said in *Doing Theology in a Revolutionary Situation:* "Jesus Christ does not come to superimpose a different, transcendent, or celestial reality on top of the realm of nature and history, but to reopen for man the will and the power to fulfill his historical vocation. He has not come to make man into superhuman beings, or a religious creature, but to open to him to the will and power to be man."[49]

Gutiérrez, and a number of other theologians of liberation who had worked with Catholic Action or similar activist groups before Vatican II, struggled with previous rationales for Christians to work at making the world a better place. Most of the largely French-inspired Catholic intellectuals and activists followed the distinction of Jacques Maritain that emphasized the autonomy of the temporal sphere from the church. In his view there were two worlds, each with its own autonomy. The church (thinking in terms of its clergy) had the task of inspiring lay persons to work in the world and seek the fulfillment of their vocations there. But the church itself was not to become directly involved. Throughout the 1950s and early 1960s the official church in places such as Brazil, Peru, Venezuela, and Bolivia became increasingly skittish about officially sanctioned Catholic Action groups' taking explicit political stands. This resulted in a break with the hierarchy, disillusionment (for a while) of clerical and lay leaders, and the eventual adoption of a new perspective on nature and grace, church and world.

Applying the insights of the unity of history meant that (Catholic) theologians of liberation and activists had no need to wait for a mandate from a bishop for activity in the political or social sphere. It was the "vocation" of all men and women to work for the construction of a just society. Gutiérrez cites Edward Schillebeeckx, the noted Dutch theologian: "The hermeneutics [meaning] of the kingdom of God consists especially in making the world a better place."[50]

Liberation thinkers have consistently emphasized the importance of the history of liberation, of the historical perspective of theology. No one has mined this area more fervently than Enrique Dussel. He has produced a number of works on the history of Latin America.[51] Dussel's writings do not center on generals and presidents; they focus on the poor and the oppressed—the way they lived and the reasons they became or remained poor and oppressed. He describes their struggles and the work of leaders such as Las Casas and the early bishops who struggled with them. And he tells of those who fought against them or did nothing. This is history from the reverse side, the underside—the side of the poor.

Dussel and other liberation theologians also emphasize that history should be used as a primary source for theology.[52] Theologians are urged to search history for facts and interpretations, no longer relying on philosophy as their paramount auxiliary.

Political Activity

The differences between Latin American and North Atlantic theologians are very evident on a third important theme of liberation theology: the call to become involved in political activity.[53] The disagreement is not about the political (public) nature of Christian presence or activity: political theology is not unknown in European circles. Rather the disagreement has to do with the level of commitment maintained by North Atlantic theologians in their discussion. Míguez Bonino argues forcefully against them:

> They want to remain at some neutral or intermediate level in which there is no need to opt for this or that concrete political praxis. We have already seen that such an attempt is self-deceptive. The opposite position which we adopt brings with it a particular risk. Nobody will claim, in fact, that his analysis of social, political, and economic reality is more than a rational exercise, open to revision, correction, or rejection.[54]

The theologians of liberation argue that to remain at the level of generality is to endorse the status quo—that is, to accept without criticism the economic and political system within which one lives.

In contrast, too, to the notion that political activity is a part-time affair, to be done alongside family life, professional life, or leisure activities, Gutiérrez argues:

> But today those who have chosen a liberating commitment find politics to be a dimension that includes and conditions all human activity. It is a global environment and collective arena of human fulfillment. Only by starting from this perception of the universality of politics in a revolutionary perspective can a more restricted sense of the term be understood, one which accurately defines politics as the orientation to political power. Every human situation has then a political dimension.[55]

This new stance carries Christians unapologetically into politics in Latin America. A number of dedicated Catholics, lay and clerical, formed part of the Nicaraguan government after the fall of Somoza. Four priests have held cabinet or high-level posts in that government.

Such a worldview also carries Latin American Christians into trouble. It brings them into conflict with governments and the military (as will be discussed in a later chapter). It also leads to misunderstanding by North Atlantic theologians and conservative church leaders in Latin America and Rome. European and North American theologians often disdain Latin American activism as another proof of the superficial and unprofessional quality of Latin American thought. Conservative, even moderate, church officials tend not to understand social and political activism, largely because they adhere to traditional models wherein church and world are separate entities with distinct histories. Implicit in their mentality is separateness of nature and grace, the natural and supernatural, what is divine and what is human.

Conflict and Change

Another difference between liberation and traditional theologians is their attitude toward conflict. Most traditional theologians assume that stability, tranquility, status quo, consensus, are the norms. This is not true for liberation theologians, for whom instability, institutionalized violence, and change are the valid concepts for interpreting what is taking place in much of Latin America. Joseph Laishley rightly cautions: "Since we are dealing with a framework of interpretation, we are not asking whether this is true or false, but whether it is more or less an adequate tool for interpreting, for making predictions and guiding action. Only constant observation and testing can prove whether it is so or not."[56]

Option for the Poor

In the original cluster of ideas developed in discussions among liberation theologians and articulated by one or another participant, one idea does not follow from another by deduction; one theme leads intuitively and easily to another. Gutiérrez's *A Theology of Liberation* exhibits a forceful unity, each theme interrelated with other themes, a network after the manner of a symmetrical spider's web. It is in this way that a fifth major theme, the option for the poor and oppressed, appears throughout the network of ideas in liberation theology. Option for the poor is the driving force in the dynamics of liberation theology.

In their reading of the struggles of Latin American peoples, liberation theologians ask, On which side of the struggle is God's preference and the presence of the church to be found? If that does not immediately sound like a theological question, at least consider it a biblical question, say liberation theologians. The unfolding of the theme of the option for the poor offers an excellent example of the workings of liberation theology. Latin America is seen as a continent suffering from external domination and internal colonialism. This is the first step, that of describing *hechos*—facts, reality. In the situation of dependence and colonialism, the majority of Latin Americans are the poor, the nonpersons—those systematically discriminated against and excluded from full participation in government services or national life.

The second step, *reflexión*—searching through sacred scripture and church teaching—reveals that God has come to the people as a liberator, championing human (material and spiritual) development. This theme is developed out of the Old and New Testaments. Theologians using scripture have a twofold task: to attempt to understand the text in its historical situation, and then to reflect on what the text says to them in their historical situation. They thereby set up a back-and-forth tension, an interplay between the text and the person reflecting. It is a hermeneutical circle, circulation "between the text in its historicity and our own historical reading of it in obedience," as Míguez Bonino explains.[57]

Robert McAfee Brown comments that this reading of the text in our own situation is no easy task, for the reading also means listening to what others have to say about our situation. We may think simply that we are living in a situation of prosperity, but others may say that our prosperity is in part due to our exploitation of them.[58]

Liberation theologians believe strongly that God takes sides—in favor of the poor, the nonpersons. Such texts as Exodus 1:8–14, 2:23–25, and 3:7–10 show that God takes the side of the poor and oppressed. The entire Old Testament can be read as a vigorous repudiation of poverty.[59] Gutiérrez offers three reasons for the repudiation of poverty. First, poverty contradicts the very meaning of Mosaic religion, the mission of liberation. Secondly, slavery and exploitation go against the mandate of Genesis: to become the subject of creative freedom that is achieved through work; to demand just treatment for the poor, slaves, and aliens. Thirdly, the human person, beyond being the image and likeness of God, is the very sacrament of God—that is, "we meet God in our encounter with men; what is done for others is done for the Lord. In a word, the existence of poverty represents a sundering both of solidarity among men and also of communion with God. Poverty is an expression of sin—that is, of a negation of love. It is therefore incompatible with the coming of the kingdom of God, a kingdom of love and justice."[60]

Others have concentrated on the New Testament. Segundo Galilea says that "the basic intuition is that in Christianity it is essential to have a sense of the poor, to opt for the poor, to serve and liberate the poor."[61] A key text is Luke 4:16–30: Jesus announces his mission to the poor and the oppressed and promises release from captivity and freedom for the oppressed. He also declares a jubilee year involving radical economic reordering.

But liberation theologians argue that the whole tenor of the New Testament is enough to emphasize the privileged position of the poor in the saving encounter with God. The poor are blessed; it is especially to them that the good news is brought. And it is among the poor, the suffering, the oppressed that the Lord is present in a very special way. Galilea continues: "In the parable of the last judgment, the liberating service of the poor (even if it is no more than material aid) is the path of salvation, and the absence of this sense of the poor, as my brothers in need, is the road to destruction."[62]

Liberation theologians make pastoral applications as their third step. A number of implications for pastoral practice (praxis) have been made in regard to the option for the poor. The most notable of them was emphasized at Puebla; indeed, some consider it to be the major achievement of that conference: the church should exercise preferential treatment for the poor and the oppressed. Secondly, the church and Christians should live a simple lifestyle. This is a theme introduced by John XXIII at Vatican II, where it was partially developed but then dropped. It was then taken up by Gutiérrez and numerous others, notably Hélder Câmara and Leonidas Proaño, bishops who practiced what they preached, and expressed as a central issue at Medellín. Thirdly, the poor and the oppressed should have the gospel preached to them in their own voice, in small communities, the grassroots Christian communities. Other implications include struggle against the excesses of capitalism and against the repressive tactics of governments that are especially hard on the poor and marginalized.

Because of its methodology, liberation theology developed a different starting point from that of traditional theology. Theoretically theology could have many starting points. Like St. Thomas and the Scholastics, one could start with nature and conclude from reasoning based on causality or order that there must be a God. This gets one as far as the God of the philosophers, but not to the God of belief. Secondly, one could follow St. Thomas further and apply teachings derived from an inerrant book or an infallible church. One thus moves from revelation to the world, on which revelation sheds its light. Thirdly, modern theologians have sometimes started with the inherently rational nature of the human mind and then concluded that a universe out of which such rationality could evolve must itself be the creation of a Supreme Mind.

Although not denying the validity of such approaches, liberation theology has its own. It takes a view from below, where the vast majority of the human family lives, "where pain is." God is to be found in the life of the poor. The God of the Jewish Testament is the God of the poor and the oppressed. God sides with them, taking their part and identifying with them. The God of the New Testament is the same God. Even more, God becomes man, not one possessed of wealth or influence but one who belonged to the poor of the land, a lower-class Jew who cast his lot with the poor.

Assmann was one of the first to talk about the epistemological privilege of the poor. He believes that the way they view the world is closer to reality than is the way the rich view it. The way the poor view the world is accurate to a degree that is impossible for those who see the world only from a vantage point of privileges they want to retain. Assmann did not have in mind the indolent poor; he was thinking of the struggling poor, those who do not accept their lot as a whim of fate or a divine decree conveniently sanctioning the status of those who hold power. This concept of the epistemological privilege of the poor gives a fuller idea of the richness of feeling and attachment that liberation theologians have for the poor.

Liberation

A sixth theme, which follows closely the idea of the option for the poor, is the explicit elaboration of the central idea of liberation. It is a very extensive theme and is approached from varying perspectives by diverse liberation theologians. Five elements can be singled out as forming the core of what liberation has come to mean in their theology: 1) sin and redemption; 2) salvation as a social event; 3) temporal liberation; 4) biblical promise; and 5) exile or captivity as the starting point.

Sin is seen not only as personal and individual: the effects of original sin are seen in social structures; they include political and economic oppression. Persons are born and live in these structures not by the direct will of God, but as a result of humankind's moral failure to construct a world of justice. Sin is not just individual deliberate irresponsibility; it is systemic evil—institutionalized injustice or systematic discrimination.

Total human redemption, then, involves not only a cleansing from individual sin but liberation from oppressive structures of the world of today. Liberation means movement toward a new age where all persons will be free, autonomous, living responsibly and with dignity in their own culture.

For many Christians (including theologians) salvation has been thought of as an individual event, usually understood as personal salvation in the afterlife, passage into full life with God. Following the insights of Vatican II and of modern theology, salvation is seen by liberation theologians as a social event, as wholeness and total social well-being in community with others.

Moreover, salvation or liberation begins to take place here and now. It is not thought of as deliverance from a fated nature. Rather, as Letty Russell describes it, it is the power and possibility of transforming the world, restoring creation, and seeking to overcome suffering.[63] Galilea adds:

> Genuinely liberating events happen in society, in history, in the lives of men: for example, a happening that brings justice to the oppressed; a political change that really creates more freedom; the power to overcome vices, chronic diseases, and so on.[64]

At Medellín the idea was characterized as "the passing of each and every one of us from less human to more human living conditions."[65]

At the heart of liberation theology is the acceptance of the idea of liberation as biblical promise. Pironio, Gutiérrez, and others substituted the term liberation for human development, in part because as they read and attempted to find meaning in sacred scripture for Latin America they believed that liberation was a much truer biblical term than development.

Some of the first formulations of liberation theology were developed out of exodus themes and Jesus's miracles. Galilea summarizes the position:

> The exodus is the people of Israel leaving the bondage of Egypt. Guided by Moses, it is led toward Palestine, the promised land, so that it may establish itself there as an independent people. The exodus is, literally, a political fact: Israel's liberation from Eyptian oppression . . . for the Israelites, it is a liberating political experience. But beyond its political significance, it has a religious meaning: the experience of God who saves, who tears his people away from the enslavement of sin, who fulfills his promise to constitute it as the chosen people.[66]

The bishops at Medellín made their own the same interpretation and application: "Just as in bygone days Israel, the first people, experienced the saving presence of God when he freed them from the bondage of Egypt, so too are we, the new people of God, bound to feel his presence."[67]

Galilea, and others, find a liberation motif in miracles:

> [They] concerned earthly liberation: loaves were multiplied to feed the hungry crowd, the sick were healed, the possessed recovered their peace of soul. But in their purpose, these miracles had a deeper and more religious significance: they were attempting to lead the Jews to the belief that the salvation promised by God was already among them. That is why in order to confirm to John that he was the Messiah and Savior, Jesus replied to John's messengers: "Go and tell John what you hear and see: the blind receive their sight and the lame walk, lepers are cleansed and the deaf hear, and the dead are raised up, and the poor have the good news preached to them."[68]

Much fuller developments of the biblical basis of liberation have been made since the first sketchy but well-argued beginnings made by Gutiérrez, Galilea, and others. One of the first areas to be developed after Gutiérrez's ground-breaking *A Theology of Liberation* was precisely the theme of Jesus as liberator.

In summary, liberation theologians have found much of the scriptures opening up to them new insights on liberation. Justo and Catherine González point out that many of the passages assigned for Sunday reading in Catholic and mainline Protestant churches lend themselves to liberation themes.[69] Space will not allow further development here of how liberation theologians are building a fuller biblical base for their interpretations but one should point out what are probably the five great liberation texts. They are called by Brown: 1) the God who takes sides (Exod. 1:8-14, 2:2-25, 3:7-10); 2) to know God is to do justice (Jer. 22:13-16); 3) true worship (Isa. 58:6-7; Amos 5:21, 2-24); 4) liberty to the oppressed (Luke 4:16-30); and 5) judgment on the nations (Matt. 25:1-46).[70]

Praxis

The discussion of the seventh of the early themes of liberation theology examined the richness of the concept of praxis. Gutiérrez and others developed the idea of orthopraxis. They enlarged the theme along several lines, two of which are particularly important. One is the idea of fidelity or integrity: that practice should match vision or beliefs. Thus the church should be more concerned about orthopraxis, instead of concentrating, as in the past, on orthodoxy, correct intellectual tenets. The second perspective was that of orthopraxis as efficacious love. Liberation theology bases itself on praxis, on a commitment to liberation. This means in practice a theology rooted in service to others, especially the neediest.

This theological theme was not meant only as a corrective to academic theology, which may hold itself apart from the real world; it was also addressed to large numbers of Latin Americans symbolized by the *beatas* of the lower classes or the *buenos católicos* of the upper class who turn their backs on the needy. The theologians felt that the Latin American church had been especially guilty in sheltering church-goers instead of challenging them. A confession of guilt was made by the church at Medellín when it described itself as "a sinful church in a sinful society." The church also made a giant step toward the poor and toward simplifying itself at Medellín, a step that turned into a leap at

Puebla when the church opted for preferential (though not exclusive) treatment for the poor.

Hope and the Kingdom

The eighth theme of the first formulations of liberation theology was similar to a theme being developed simultaneously in many other parts of the world, that of hope and the coming of the kingdom (eschatology). As a central theme it appears in Gutiérrez's *A Theology of Liberation* (1971), James Cone's *Theology of Black Liberation* (1973), and Letty Russell's *Human Liberation in a Feminist Perspective* (1974). In Russell the theme is a conscious elaboration of the European theology of hope of Jürgen Moltmann and the political theology of Johannes Metz. Although considerable debt is owed by Gutiérrez and others to this European influence, Latin Americans have tried to distance themselves from Metz and Moltmann. The debate became especially strong between two Protestant theologians, Moltmann and Míguez Bonino, both highly influential in international circles. The debate is too lengthy to be discussed here.[71] It will suffice to recount some of the main outlines of the concept of hope and the coming of the kingdom as developed by Latin American liberation theologians.

Here another fount of influence on Latin American liberation thought must be mentioned: North American liberal Protestantism. As yet this history has not been written or even fully documented. Influence, moreover, has been mutual and it is difficult at times to judge which partner, North or South America, gained more in the interchange of ideas. It will be enough here to say that financial and intellectual support for Latin America from the National Council of Churches has been substantial and steady over a period of fifteen years. Two U.S. schools of theology, Union (New York) and Princeton, have been especially active in the interchange of ideas with Latin American theologians. One of the most notable Latin American Protestant theologians involved in this interchange is Rubem Alves, a Brazilian who has been active as a pioneer of liberation thought. His is the first major formulation of a theology of hope in Latin America.[72]

For Alves the underlying question of his life and work has been,

What is necessary for forming and conserving human life in the
world? For him the answer is "our vocation to freedom." His
position is similar to that of John Courtney Murray, perhaps the
greatest U.S. Catholic theologian in this century, who said in
1965, "The first truth about man is that he is free, so that the first
truth about Christ is that he is liberator, the one through whom
man is set free."[73]

Alves and others evolved a theology of hope as a second step
("moment") after reflecting on the Latin American, especially
the Brazilian, situation of the late 1960s. (Recall that torture and
repression were systematically applied to dissidents in Brazil after
1968.) In reflecting on this situation, Alves and others searched
the scriptures. Increasingly the central thought of the kingdom of
God lost its far-away, after-life character for them. They began to
realize that the kingdom as presented in the synoptic gospel writers (Matthew, Mark, and Luke) was to be realized *now*, building
toward the future. Thus the present and future tasks of the Christian became much more emphasized by liberation theologians
than a retelling of the past. Gutiérrez especially felt that Latin
American Christianity had given far too much emphasis to its
past.

In shorthand terms, one may say that liberation theologians
emphasized such ideas as realizing the future, making the
kingdom present now. In this they were clearly opting for a
theology that includes utopia as a central part of its vision. "Utopia" was meant in the sense of working for a better future society,
one that would not be fully realized before the end of time. Nonetheless there was an "inner" mandate, one of the laws of the gospel and of life, that human beings should work actively for a
society in which more just relationships would prevail.

Thus liberation theology in its first formulations came full circle to the first and second themes (unity of history and the political dimension of religion): religiously motivated men and women
work actively in human/religious history to construct a more
equitable society, a work that necessarily involves politics because
all human activity has a political dimension. Other themes enter
naturally to complete the movement: concretely, the building of
the kingdom (just society) means preferential (but not exclusive)
treatment of the poor and oppressed, working for their liberation

(freedom from unjust restraints in order for them to achieve their full human/Christian potential). Fidelity to a Christian vocation will be measured by orthopraxis (efficacious love) more than by orthodoxy. Although the theological "movements," or themes, of the original formulations appear in a circular pattern, the theologians themselves prefer to think in terms of a spiral; a circle is static and fixed, a poor symbol for life.

Later Themes

Christology

In his central work, *A Theology of Liberation*, Gutiérrez outlines a number of unfinished tasks for liberation theologians. Chief among them, in terms of immediate needs, were more elaborated works on christology and spirituality. As to the first area, liberation theologians were acutely aware of the necessity of showing the specifically Christian character of their work. This they needed to head off their many critics, some of whom superficially wrote them off as half-baptized Marxists playing in the intellectual garden of Ernst Bloch (humanistic Marxism). Further, given the personalistic character of Latin American culture, the liberation theologians would gain few adherents without appeal to the life and personality of Christ. However, one has only to read the works on Jesus the liberator that followed Gutiérrez's work to realize the deep personal conviction of the authors as to the centrality of Christ in the liberation process.

Jon Sobrino and Leonardo Boff produced the two first major works in liberation christology.[74] Both have fared better in the high seas of North Atlantic theological criticism than a number of other liberation works. Their writings have depth of scholarship and forceful argumentation that reflect the extensive European training of their authors. Their influence and that of other liberation theologians working in christology was evident at Puebla where christology suffuses the final document (unlike the Medellín document).

The most important christological work in liberation theology (understood in the larger sense of any theology developing the liberation theme regardless of geographical region) has been produced by a European, Edward Schillebeeckx. His *Jesus: An Experiment in Christology*[75] and *Christ: The Experience of Jesus as Lord*[76] display a breadth of scholarship, especially biblical scholarship, unmatched by most modern theologians. They also exhibit the same methodological steps as Latin American liberation theology. Schillebeeckx is one of the leading theologians of the world; the close similarity between his work and that of the Latin American liberation theologians offers major reinforcement for their work.

Spirituality

Another criticism fired at the early liberation theologians was their lack of concern for spirituality. The neo-Marxist character of some of their formulations, the secular emphasis of their thought, and especially the lack of extended discussion on the spiritual nature of Christianity left liberation theologians vulnerable to criticism—especially from fellow Latin Americans whose religion was nothing if not other-worldly. Gutiérrez recognized this lack. In *A Theology of Liberation* he states that one of the reasons for it was not an absence of desire or practice but of intellectual development of the theme: "If they [activist Christians] are not always able to express in appropriate terms the profound reasons for their commitment, it is because the theology in which they were formed—and which they share with other Christians—has not produced the categories necessary to produce this option"; this foreshadows Gutiérrez's full-length statement of a spirituality of liberation in: *We Drink from Our Own Wells*."[77]

No one has thus far responded more deeply and thoroughly to this lack than Segundo Galilea. In three works, *El sentido del pobre*, *Apostolado y contemplación*, and *Vivir el cristianismo*, Galilea planted the seeds of a spirituality of liberation.[78] This spirituality was then developed more systematically in his *Espiritualidad de la liberación*.[79] He enlarges upon five ideas as basic to a new spirituality, one in contrast to monastic or traditional spirituality. First, change of heart, conversion, is realized through a commitment, a conversion to other human beings. Secondly, the so-called history of salvation is intimately related to the history of the liberation of the poor. Thirdly, tasks and commitments involved in the liberation process anticipate the kingdom of God. Fourthly, charity (love) takes its historical form in liberation praxis. Fifthly, Latin Americans should attempt a reading of the beatitudes specifically for Latin America. This would be a reading done by the poor on a continent of the poor.

Another liberation theologian who has devoted his attention to spirituality from a liberation point of view is Jon Sobrino. His writing on prayer has found an appreciative audience. Sobrino also took part with other liberation theologians in a groundbreaking attempt of seven Latin American journals of religious thought that culminated in a publishing enterprise devoted to the theme of spirituality of liberation. This cooperative effort on the part of liberation theologians and their publishers characterizes much of what has been taking place in Latin America: a sense of urgency, dialogue (stemming from eagerness to learn from others), evolutionary development, dialectical growth, and flexible, well-planned, efficient cooperation.

Ecclesiology

Another major area of theology opened up by Gutiérrez is ecclesiology.[80] He pointed out the central place of the church in the salvation/liberation process but he did not systematically develop the theme. Others, such as Segundo and Boff, have produced fuller theological treatments of the church.[81] Liberation theologians are in the field "doing church" and have settled in their own minds what "church" should be: *comunidades eclesiales de base*, grassroots Christian communities. This is the reality, the praxis, out of which they do their theology. It is also the reality out of which the future of the Latin American church will dawn. It is appropriate, then, that when Boff elaborates the rationale for grassroots communities he entitles the book *Ecclesiogénesis* ("the church coming to life").

Biblical Basis

A final point about the content of liberation theology should be made, especially for the benefit of those for whom the Bible is the centerpiece for faith and for doing theology. Liberation theologians are of the same opinion. But there are few direct treatments of the Bible by scripture scholars from a liberation perspective. In a sense the theologians are outrunning the exegetes. Liberation theology is a major step in the interaction of biblical and theological scholars, an interaction that has been taking place since the birth of modern biblical studies, beginning at the time of World War I.

Catholic and Protestant biblical scholarship currently enjoys a reputation for high academic standards and achievements. However, liberation theologians fault many modern exegetes for their hermeneutics, or interpretations, saying that they know the literal meaning of the text but that they do not know what the text means in our times.[82] This flaw derives from two sources: biblical scholars until rather recently did not pay much attention to the sociology of the bible, the socio-economic context of biblical happenings, and they did not ask the right questions of the text.

Thus one has only to look up modern interpretations of what the poor mean in the New Testament, taking "blessed are the poor" or similar texts. New Testament commentators almost unanimously denied that Jesus had the literally poor in mind; they held out for the poor in spirit. There have been a few exceptions among older biblical scholars and now a major shift to a liberation perspective is taking place among younger biblical commentators, in large part due to the challenge offered by liberation theologians.

Achievements

The crowning achievement of liberation theology is methodological. Liberation theologians have perfected and put into active practice the methodology used by Vatican II in *Gaudium et Spes*. This methodology has brought them and the church into the daily lives and problems of the peoples of Latin America in a way that traditional theology had not accomplished in four hundred years. As a result, the Latin American church will never be the same again.

The second major achievement is emphasis on and elaboration of the relationship between Christian faith and the struggle for justice in the world. During the 1960s official documents of both

Catholic and Protestant church bodies made it very clear that the struggle to achieve a decent existence for the suffering majority of humankind was the embodiment of Christian love in the world. The official teaching has been taken up with great enthusiasm in the so-called Third World. From now on it is expected that the churches of the Third World will offer strong leadership within larger church bodies. Walbert Bühlmann remarks that we may even have a Lima I instead of a Vatican III.[83]

A third major achievement has occurred in the area of ecumenism. In various parts of the world there has been progress in mutual understanding and movement toward unification. But in the Third World there is a parallel path toward unity on the level of orthopraxis—that is, de facto commitment by Christians. Their common struggle has united them very deeply. Alfred Hennelly remarks that the last great division among the Christian churches may involve a gulf separating those who read the gospel as a summons to the struggle for justice and those who are indifferent or even hostile to such an interpretation.[84]

A fourth achievement is the intimate relationship that has been established between theology and Christian praxis throughout parts of the Third World. All the writings mentioned above have arisen out of praxis and are intended to enhance praxis. The result is liberation evangelization for millions on the grassroots level.

A fifth achievement is that we have been shown that theology can be a communal effort. Theology of liberation is not the system of a single person, a Rahner or Tillich, a de Chardin or Barth; it is rather a cooperative effort of many. At least as a symbol, liberation theology represents Christianity well, for it is the joint effort of men and women of all skin colors working throughout the world on a common project which is aimed at building up a society of justice and love. Rather than competition, there is sharing of ideas. Liberation theologians know one another, respect one another, and promote their ideas. This is unusual at least in some parts of Latin America, where misanthropy is known to run high. Theology, thus seen, is a communal effort, confronting a common catastrophe.[85]

The fad that will not go away, Latin American theology of liberation, has influenced theologians and activists in other countries and has helped to spawn other theologies of liberation. The first areas of the world where that influence was noted were Africa and Asia. African and Asian theologians have not copied liberation theology directly but rather have adopted a similarity of style or approach to Christian reflection on what is taking place in Africa and Asia. Kosuke Koyama's *No Handle on the Cross* or Allan Boesak's *Farewell to Innocence* read like Asian and African inventions rather than Latin American imitations.[86]

The network of liberation theologians widened to include theologians from Africa and Asia in the Ecumenical Association of Third World Theologians (EATWOT). Their first meeting at Dar es Salaam in 1976 demonstrated the influence of the Latin Americans and also showed areas of basic agreement, such as in method and theological objectives.[87] The Africans took the initiative of forming their own regional group, so that a Pan-African conference was held in Ghana in 1977. It was evident that Third World theology was beginning to thrive in other parts of the world.

As liberation theology was developing in Latin America out of theologians' social experience, so too was black and feminist liberation theology in the United States. Gutiérrez's *Notas para una teología de la liberación* was presented at a conference in 1968. James Cone's *A Black Theology of Liberation* (1970) was followed by J. Deotis Roberts's *Liberation and Reconciliation: A Black Theology* (1971), Frederick Herzog's *Liberation Theology* (1972), Letty M. Russell's *Ferment of Freedom* (1972) and *Human Liberation in a Feminist Perspective* (1974), and Rosemary Radford Reuther's *Liberation Theology* (1973). A number of other works including many by North American theologians who are neither black nor female have followed this initial outburst, indicating the long-lasting appeal that liberation theology has exercised.

Informal contacts between North and Latin American theologians have been maintained for a long time. Some of these contacts were stimulated through yearly meetings of CICOP sponsored by the Latin American Office of the U.S. Catholic Conference. The 1971 meeting was the last and perhaps the most important: it had as its theme the theology of liberation. It thereby introduced many in the U.S.A. to the ideas that were in ferment in

Latin America[88] and that would be focused in Gutiérrez's central work, which appeared in English translation two years later.

Following a massive conference in Mexico City in 1975, attended by almost every Latin American theologian of note, some of the leading Latin Americans went north to Detroit for the first formal meeting of Theology in the Americas.[89] A frank interchange took place and sparks flew over differences in perspectives between the Latin Americans and some of their counterparts in black, feminist, or Chicano liberation theology. Nonetheless, interaction continues.

Detroit II was held in the summer of 1980.[90] It was preceded by the fourth international of EATWOT in São Paulo, to which representatives from the U.S.A. and Europe were invited for the first time.[91] The fifth EATWOT conference, centered on dialogue between Third World and First World theologians, was held in Geneva, Switzerland, in January 1983.[92]

Theology in the Americas itself represents an interesting case in ecumenism. It is an office housed at the headquarters of the National Council of Churches (historical Protestant churches) and was run until August 1980 by Sergio Torres, a Chilean priest, and continues through the coordinating activities of two Catholic sisters, Caridad Guidote and Margaret Coakley.

It would be too lengthy to trace here the influence and interaction of Latin American theologians with those of Western Europe except to say that interaction varies widely from country to country.[93] Differences of opinion are most intense on the part of some German theologians, whereas many Spanish theologians appear much more open to liberation theology. Meetings of Latin American theologians with their Spanish colleagues took place at El Escorial in 1972 and at Toledo in 1974. The interchange of ideas has continued, Ignacio González Faus, editor of the review *Selecciones de Teología*, being one of its key figures.

In summary, with such international influence, liberation theology is not a trend that will fade away before the next meeting of the Catholic Theology Society of America. Liberation theology is entrenched in official church documents; it lives and breathes in the lives of numerous small communities.

4

A New Social Structure: Grassroots Christian Communities

Traditional Catholics consider grassroots Christian communities outrageous innovations. Military regimes in Brazil, Argentina, and Paraguay monitor them closely. Historical Protestant churches are pleased with their development and consider them a step in their direction. The Latin American Catholic Church itself responded at Puebla: "We are happy to single out the multiplication of small communities as an important ecclesial event that is peculiarly ours, and as the 'hope of the church.' "[1]

Many influences on the Latin American church converge in the creation of *comunidades de base*; they are profoundly Latin American in their origination. They are also very numerous: some two to three million Latin American Catholics (one million of them in Brazil) take part in these communities. For many participants the experience is so intense that they live their lives largely on the basis of their commitment to the community and to the church.[2]

Basic Christian communities are like living cells in an organism newly coming to life. Generally, twelve to twenty persons make up a community. They usually come together in their neighborhood or village once a week. They read sacred scripture, pray together, and sing hymns. They reflect on what the scriptures mean in their daily lives. That reflection frequently leads them to courses of political action to improve the living conditions in their barrio. Given the repressive political climate in many Latin American countries, such actions have sometimes resulted in jailings, deaths, and disappearances (persons are taken to a police station, for example, and are never seen again).

The impact of the basic Christian communities has been enormous on the church and on other sectors of society. For the church they have meant movement at the grass roots, something long overdue and largely unexpected. "If someone had told me twenty years ago that I would be witnessing Catholics, ordinary ones, reading the Bible and caring for one another on the basis of scriptural reflection, and doing this in large numbers, I would have told them they were seriously misled," remarked Reverend William Wipfler, an Episcopalian priest who has been studying the Latin American church for many years.

This major innovation in the life of the Latin American church has distinctive facets that will be discussed in this chapter: social factors that brought the communities to life, new theological emphasis on the local church, types of mature communities, their day-by-day activities, their connection with liberation theology, their political character (with the particular issue of land tenure).

Roots of the New Communities

The communities arose from a variety of factors, many of which converged at the time of Vatican II and in its aftermath. Most innovations begin with dissatisfactions; so too the creation of the base communities. The immense parishes of the Latin American church, with as many as eighty thousand nominal members, were increasingly recognized as unmanageable organizational units. Priests left the organization, to some extent because of the impossibility of their task. One Brazilian priest wrote earnestly to his parishioners that Catholics were killing their priests with their demands.[3]

Many of these demands were for ritualistic services without much meaning. For some it was clearly a matter of magic, superstition. Even among those who had a more enlightened attitude, questions arose about the "service station" approach, one that had Catholics coming to a *patrón* who dispensed favors and services. Further questions were raised by Vatican II about conferring sacraments on those who had almost no instruction. Indeed many came to believe that emphasis on performing ecclesiastical rites was the curse of the Latin American church.

To respond to the situation several major changes were called for: reduction in scale, instruction in depth, a sense of community, new ministries, and emergence of lay leaders. All this seemed new but reflection on the social environment, emphasis on community, and lay leadership were foreshadowed by lay movements in Latin America that preceded Vatican II and supposedly abrupt changes that took place thereafter.

Some observers have felt that the church had no choice but to found (or allow) grassroots communities. With so few priests and a growing population—90 percent nominally Catholic—the church had to decentralize and welcome lay persons as leaders. But the shortage of priests was not the only, or even the major, reason for the emergence of base communities: the church in many places had been lacking in clergy for decades. Additional factors are needed to explain the birth of the grassroots communities and the direction they have taken.

José Marins, a key figure in the spread of the base communities, recalls that beginning in the 1950s and more evidently in the 1960s priests working in various parts of Latin America began feeling the malaise that comes from working with a parish structure that was out of alignment with pastoral ideology. The parish structure was not achieving the results that enlightened pastors sought. Marins,[4] Aldo Gerna,[5] both in Brazil, and Leo Mahan[6] in Panama began experimenting with alternative parish structures. Their description of the process enlightens one also about the education that took place in the priests themselves. Pastors began by talking with the people, largely to gain support for what the priests had in mind. Little by little they found themselves listening with fewer preconceptions and then acting on the needs expressed by the people.

The same kinds of experimental structures began appearing in isolated parts of Latin America. The innovations were not always spontaneous, for by now communication across diocesan or national lines had very much improved. Experiments were observed and adapted elsewhere. Priests and bishops looking for innovations heard Leo Mahan describe at CICOP meetings the workings of San Miguelito parish in Panama City or they dropped in to see for themselves what was happening there. (Much of the air traffic to and from Latin America passed through Panama.) Theologian Francisco Bravo came to study the parish; Illich's documentation center printed and circulated his report.

The most evident need for change in structure was reduction in scale. Worshipers found it virtually impossible to relate to strangers in a large church building amid mysterious rites. So the first change that practically all innovators made was to reduce the church community to the smallest human scale. This amounted to the natural grouping one finds in a subneighborhood or village, a grouping of persons who live within a block or two of one another. After further experimentation most communities limited themselves to adults, at least as the most active participants. Over and over pioneer community leaders explained that young children and adolescents were not ready for the communities: "Everyone has to assume mature commitment to one another and the younger ones are not ready."

Membership: Adult and Poor

The concentration on adults represented a major shift in the church's approach to its goals. For decades the majority of the church's educational efforts had been aimed at young children or adolescents through schools or catechetical programs. The church would now attempt to reach children through their parents. Whatever the weakness of this strategy—given the lack of theological training for most adults—the approach has the advantage of being "natural" (parents teaching their own children) and of rapidly multiplying the number of pastoral ministers. The approach also gives the church a more mature image. "Previously we were a church of old ladies and young children. I was ashamed as a young man to take part in such an enterprise," recalled a lay leader from northeast Brazil.[7]

The experimentation also laid to rest the "myth of the passive peasant." From the beginning it was clear that there were natural leaders in the groups. At the start of the base community movement many of the priest-innovators selected the leaders; now typically the groups elect the leaders, followed by ratification by the pastor or bishop, usually in a simple ceremony. "These people know one another. They know who can be trusted, who will not lord it over them, and who will move them along without too much friction. Only a very few times have they chosen somebody who turned out to be lazy or unreliable," remarked Father Ralph Rogawski, who has organized base communities in Latin America and the U.S.A.[8]

Many basic communities developed in rural areas, though some can be found in the barrios of cities, as in Cali, Lima, and especially São Paulo. Most participants are rural indigents, *campesinos*, or have recently migrated to cities. For many members, a base community gave them their first significant contact with Christianity. Few received religious instruction in any systematic manner, though a number had on occasion listened to religious programing from the numerous radio schools that have sprung up in the last twenty years in Latin America. Very few members had read the Bible for themselves.

In terms of social background the vast majority of grassroots community members are rural or urban working-class poor. Few participants belong to the "educated" middle class and even fewer are from the upper class. There are push-pull factors in this social selection. The Latin American church believes that it must give preferential treatment to the poor, especially those on the margins of society. As Rogawski has said:

> These have been the most neglected historically and it was our duty to readjust our pastoral priorities. There is probably another reason why the base community approach works so well with people who are or who were recently peasants. These people have a spontaneity and a hunger for learning that is missing in other social groups.[9]

Moreover, the community-based cultural orientation of many *campesinos* disposed them toward working and sharing in small groups.

External factors also affected the reordering of pastoral priorities. Among the unchurched *campesinos* and slum dwellers, sects of various kinds and old-line Pentecostals were making their greatest gains. The loyalties of the poor were under attack.

Other specific factors, already touched on above, inclined the church to its emphasis on working with the poor. The social analysis done for the Medellín and Puebla conferences pointed out the worsening situations of the lower classes. And the bishops' own sense of the people, derived from daily interviews and contacts, disposed them toward seeking innovative changes for the masses.

Shift to Local Church

Once the process of assimilating Vatican II and the new theology behind it was advancing, changes in perspective began taking shape. And myths began to evaporate. Instead of thinking of Latin America as a Catholic region in which it was necessary above all to baptize everyone, instead of worrying about everyone's receiving all the rites, the church, at least its intellectual leadership members, began emphasizing personal commitment (something closely akin to the Evangelical idea of a decision for Christ). In gross terms it meant a shift from quantity to quality.

The new theology emphasized the unity of history, that there are not two worlds, religious and secular. Nor was it necessary for all to be baptized: persons of good will are not excluded from the kingdom of God. Moreover the this-worldly emphasis of Vatican II in building up the world as a preeminently Christian work eased the Latin American church away from some of its fatalistic, otherworldly inclinations. Some of the barnacles of time were being stripped away.

The impact of these ideas would result in new corporate goals. In sum, major objectives would include: instruction in depth, direct use of the Bible, a sense of community, new ministries, the emergence and empowerment of the laity, and emphasis on working at the side of the poor. Grassroots Christian communities fulfill to one degree or another all these objectives. Above all, they bring members a sense that the church is community, not hierarchy. "We say over and over that the base communities are not associations or clubs within the church; they are the church," says José Marins.[10] The weakest achievement of the communities, though, has been training of leaders. As a result, even though members have gained familiarity with the Bible (many have worn out their copies), some base communities tend to develop fundamentalism, at least in the initial stage. "They tend to get over this biblicism, though," judged Archbishop Críspulo Benítez of Barquisimento, Venezuela, after a dozen years of watching the groups operate in his diocese.[11] Other observers are not as sanguine.

Evangelization emerged as an overriding corporate goal at Vatican II. The church in the U.S.A. is still struggling with formulation of ways by which to accomplish "making Christ known." The Latin American church was ready to respond by the time of the Medellín conference: base communities were seen as the preferred strategy. This was reinforced at the Puebla conference, which emphasized base communities throughout its final document.

Types of Base Communities

One reason confusion has grown up about the *comunidades de base* was their imprecise description as they developed historically. This has sometimes resulted in gross overcounting of communities. In some places priests say that many base communities exist in their parishes—but they are counting every conceivable religious organization. The pastor of a parish with eighty-thousand members in São Paulo divided it into four sections and called each section a base community.

Historically base communities developed from three different orientations. The first is the post-Medellín type; it has been described above and is best depicted in the writings of José Marins. The second is the group of Catholics (sometimes together with Protestants) who are part of the pentecostal or charismatic movement. The third is the catechumenate, a much less prevalent form, developed recently in Spain.

Catholic pentecostalism spread in Latin America like fire through a dry field.[12] It was introduced by enthusiasts from a number of non–Latin American countries, but the most influential came from the U.S.A. Francis MacNutt with two Methodist ministers, Joe Pietrie and Tommy Tyson, traveled in 1969 to Peru and Bolivia to begin the movement. They addressed themselves first to groups of twenty to thirty priests and sisters who could understand English. Many of them in turn began using charismatic prayer, Bible study, and sometimes healing among their parishioners and friends. Now no one knows how many Catholic pentecostals there are in Latin America. Estimates range into the millions. The growing number of persons attending local congresses (50,000 at Barquisimeto, Venezuela) or of regional representatives at international congresses (several thousand) speaks for itself.

The charismatic movement allows for greater numbers and less structuralization than do the post-Medellín or catechumenate communities. For example, in Santa Cruz, the second largest city in Bolivia, four thousand persons assemble for services at La Mansión. But more typically they come together as smaller Bible and prayer groups (20 to 75 persons), similar in most outward aspects to the type of community promoted by Marins but "adding a bit of fire and zest," as some commentators have said.

The charismatics have become a major new movement in the life of the Latin American church. Many bishops have joined the movement or welcome it into their dioceses. "I do not agree with some of its emphases but it is hard to criticize the changes the movement has brought about in the lives of many," one bishop said to me.[13] Many adherents believe the movement appeals to the innate religious sense that Latin Americans are believed to harbor. "We are an expressive people and we need an expressive religion, not the cold and distant formalism one finds in most parish churches," claimed a long-standing pentecostal member in Santa Cruz.[14]

Pentecostalism provides another transnational network for religious leadership groups in Latin America. These newer groups are typically distinct from the older intellectual or activist leadership groups. The pentecostal network reaches back and forth from Latin America to the U.S.A. and Canada. It embraces Catholics and Protestants almost interchangeably. After the beginnings of the movement at Cochabamba (Bolivia) and Lima, MacNutt and others from the charismatic movement in the U.S.A. traveled to various parts of Latin America. Leadership then passed quickly to Latin Americans. They too joined the network that expanded to include Europe and much of the Third World.

Pentecostals are world travelers but they are not, by and large, world citizens. They are widely criticized for their otherworldly spiritualism. Father Alfonso Via Reque of Cochabamba said to me:

> The world could be going to hell in a basket and these birds wouldn't notice it, much less do anything about it. When I asked a prominent charismatic about the coup in Bolivia (that of García Meza) and its bloody, terrible aftermath, the charismatic replied that the coup was a good thing. It gave Bolivia stability.[15]

Stability and peace are words frequently used by charismatics. What political involvement they enter into tends to be on the conservative side (although not to the extent of U.S. evangelicals). Thus charismatics are seen by some church administrators as "safe."

The third type of base community, the catechumenate, is a revival of one of the oldest practices of Christianity. Early Christians devised it as intense preparation and examination for baptism. The main difference is that modern participants are already baptized. In essence the catechumenate provides intensive value-education for adults.

The form varies slightly from place to place but in general follows the model developed in Spain in the last ten years. A small group of adults, usually with a priest or some other adult educator present, meets weekly for a minimum of two years. Intense instruction and commitment form the heart of the movement. "We want people to see Jesus in an adult manner and we want them to respond with a commitment. The whole point of the catechumenate is making the promise to live as a Christian with all that means for an adult," remarked Father Francisco Quijano of Mexico City.[16]

To facilitate the *compromiso* (commitment), group members begin to make themselves known little by little to other members of the group and to reflect openly on their values. This they do in view of what they have been reading together in sacred scripture and of what they have been hearing from the instructor. As time goes on, they come to a point where they challenge one another gently about apparent discrepancies between alleged values and actual behavior.

Thus far the groups are not numerous but they have been relatively effective at what they set out to accomplish. "I'd rather have one person from this program than ten charismatics," reflected Quijano. "For one thing persons from the catechumenate have a profoundly social consciousness." The catechumenate also tends to attract persons who are educated and middle-income couples. In their case the catechumenate has become a specialized *comunidad de base* for the middle class.

Functioning of Base Communities

Because the *comunidades de base* are grassroots innovations, they tend to vary from diocese to diocese and from parish to parish. But there is enough similarity among them to describe them in common terms. They are something like a regional dish that is immediately recognized as *paella* but varies from cook to cook. In many ways the modus operandi of base communities follows traditional Catholic Action models. It is only a slight exaggeration to say, as Ralph della Cava suggests, that *comunidades de base* are Catholic Action for the masses.[17]

Community leaders are the key to the continuity and dynamism of the communities. Their titles and functions vary somewhat from place to place. Some dioceses refer to community leaders as *presidentes*, those who preside over the Bible services, which are thought of as an alternative to the Mass. In the Dominican Republic the Santiago de los Caballeros diocese alone has empowered five hundred such assembly presidents. In Brazil in the late 1950s Don Angelo Rossi, one of the pioneers of the basic Christian communities, introduced the term *coordinadores* (coordinators). Several hundred coordinators assemble neighborhood or village residents at least once a week for religious instruction. They pray with the people almost daily. On Sundays and holy days they help communities to follow spiritually and collectively the liturgy that their pastor is celebrating many kilometers away in the main parish church. At various times the coordinator leads morning and evening prayers, May devotions, and the like.

Other dioceses prefer to call leaders *animadores* or *respons-*

ables, those who made sure that everyone attends and who start the discussion on the scriptural selection and keep it moving. The group thinks of itself more in terms of a study group than an alternative to the eucharistic celebration. Leaders may also define their role as leading the group to action. In many regions base community leaders emphasize the "celebration of the Word" and call their leaders "delegates (or "ministers") of the Word," or a similar title. They lead the group by helping to explain scriptural texts and by exhorting the members to follow what are proposed as Christian values.

The number of persons who act as leaders within the base communities varies widely and has implications for the life of the group and for administrative supervision from above. In Santiago de los Caballeros one person is named president. He is trained over a number of months and is formally designated by the bishop. In other places two or three couples are elected from the group as leaders for the year and will rotate weekly to bring the group together and direct meetings.

Evolution of Base Communities and Liberation Theology

As time progresses the base community achieves more of a life of its own. At the beginning, outsiders come to a village or sub-neighborhood. They recruit members, set up Bible study-prayer meetings, contribute heavily to the discussions following the scripture readings, and in general breathe life into the group. As local leadership emerges, outsiders recede further into the background, supporting by their presence the continuation of the group but contributing less to the Bible discussion or to the agenda of things to be done. Rogawski and his team, who have organized base communities in Bolivia, Colombia, Venezuela, Utah, and Texas, estimate that outside intervention is needed for periods ranging from a month to three months, presuming the outsiders live in the village or neighborhood. Other organizers, especially in remote areas, have stayed as long as five years.

Rather than moving from place to place, most organizers invite future community leaders to a central place where they can get to know other more advanced leaders and can receive instruction in Christian teaching, group method, and sometimes community development. Throughout Latin America training centers are springing up to furnish religious instruction that can be passed on to group members back home. Sample sermon or Bible lesson plans are gone over for trainees who can read. Those who cannot read have to rely on memory; some observers consider this a hazardous undertaking with a message as complex as that of Christianity.

The teachings that community leaders pass on are not complex statements of theologians but a series of simple stories. These stories of the life of the Jews and of the life of Jesus furnish a basis for members to reflect on their own values and the direction their lives are taking. The stories also speak to them about a sense of belonging and about caring for one another.

Every message has ideological overtones, although many bishops at Puebla tried to deny it. They were chided by Bishop Germán Schmitz of Lima: "Let him who is without ideology cast the first stone."[18] The theology of liberation frames and colors the message that many base communities receive. It undergirds the reflection in these groups as thoroughly as it did the Puebla conference.

For their part, liberation theologians often work closely with base communities and elaborate their theology while immersed in the lives of the community members.

Base communities frequently use concepts developed in liberation theology. They interpret the exodus as applying to them. They read Amos about helping the widow and the orphaned. And they reflect on Jesus as the one who came to liberate them. They are quick to catch on that liberation is more than spiritual. Often their discussion centers on not having to live in the unfavorable conditions that they once thought unchangeable. Health, education, and landownership become topics of reflection, replacing resignation and suffering, as in the past.

Perhaps more important than the use of liberation content, many base communities follow the liberation methodology: facts, reflection, action. "Such a method is dynamic; it can get its followers into trouble. But we try to teach them to reach out for the feasible. We also favor the nonviolent," commented Father Matías Mueller, a longtime advisor to base communities in Bolivia.[19]

Communities typically go through stages of evolution. At first most resources in terms of leadership and content come from outside. Then leadership emerges from within the community and the group finds itself relatively self-sufficient, except for upgrading its rudimentary knowledge of the Bible and Christianity. Stronger communities eventually find themselves reaching out.

Political Involvement

Communities reach out in a number of ways. First they take on the task of helping to start other communities. They feel that they should share the great gifts they have received: a sense of community and a knowledge that God shares their life. This kind of reaching out assures the spread of the community movement. The significance of this dynamic process is not lost on bishops and priests who are witnessing self-stimulating growth at the grass roots, a major change in the Latin American church.

Many communities, especially those with a charismatic orientation, limit themselves to such an outreach. But other groups are developing an outreach that is social and political. They animate the village or the barrio to build a school, to repair a road, or to dig a well. Some communities act as catalysts for labor union activity or for advocacy in political systems. They become political brokers, advocates, and campaigners ("agitators," say some military governments).

Community members join or help to create other political or economic organizations, such as labor unions, cooperatives, or agrarian leagues. (Base community members were especially influential in promoting union activity in São Paulo.) To the charge that base communities are political enterprises, their promoters reply that it is true only indirectly. They argue that other bodies (unions, for example) are needed to mediate between the demands of the people and the political system. But in situations where intermediate structures are partially or fully nonoperational— because of a repressive political environment—church bodies, such as base communities, become the only vehicles for mediating political demands.

Although these communities were founded ostensibly for religious purposes, they can serve other ends. Moreover, some—

perhaps many—who join grassroots Christian communities do so because the base communities are practically the only viable voluntary organization they could join. For at least some members these communities are their surrogate political party—that is, lacking political parties or labor unions, Christians found an outlet for their political instincts or explicit political philosophies in the base communities.

At this stage the hypothesis that base communities are little but surrogate political organizations is unproven. What it would take to test the thesis convincingly would be cessation of repression. Would there still be as many members in the base communities if there were active political parties and labor unions not hamstrung by repressive governments? Those who have watched for years the development of basic Christian communities, such as Thomas Bruneau, admit that some participants join and instinctively use the communities as a surrogate political party or labor union.[20] There should be no surprise about this. Many Latin Americans are conditioned by their culture to use practically any forum for political expression. And human beings have been using religion for their own purposes since the beginning of time.

Bruneau and other observers do not attempt to estimate the number of political "operators" to be found in base communities. Instead they point out that the vast majority of persons who join these communities are rural or urban working poor with naive, largely fatalistic, conceptions of politics. Indeed it was the prevalence of apathy in Brazil that led Paulo Freire to develop his philosophy and method of conscientization.

Base communities serve an important indirect political end: they are developing a whole generation of Latin Americans in leadership skills. These skills can be transferred, for the most part, to other spheres. Thus the ability to think on one's feet, to lead discussions, to take positions and defend them, to attempt community problem-solving, to act as advocates or mediators, or to administer larger social units than the family—all these are skills that can be applied directly in the political arena. The existence of such resources on a widespread basis means a new day dawning for the church.

The workings of base communities and their convergence with liberation theology and with political activity has been witnessed by James Pitt at São Mateus, Brazil:

The theme of that fortnight was "that Jesus was born poor and humble and shares our life," and the question was "Why?" The eight women present were all poor. None had much formal education. Most were migrants from rural areas. All knew real hardship. They could easily identify with a poor family on the move whose baby had been born in a stable. Indeed a one-minute reading of Luke's account of the nativity provoked a one-hour discussion of the injustices, humiliations, and hardships that the mothers themselves experienced.

They discussed the terrible health services available in the area and how a local woman's baby had been born while she was waiting in queue to see the doctor. (The baby died.) They swapped accounts of having to wait in shops while better dressed people were served first and how as domestic servants they were treated without respect by their mistresses. They talked of the high cost of food in the local shops.

After an hour the catechist put the question, "Why did Jesus choose to be born poor and humble?" "Maybe," said one woman, a mother of ten of whom three had died and only two were working, "maybe it was to show these rich people that we are important too. . . ."

A ripple of excitement went through the room. Was God really making such a clear statement about *their* humanity? About *their* rights as [persons]? The discussion progressed, but with an electric charge in the air. Half an hour later, a young woman said: "I think we still haven't got the right answer to the first question." A complete hush. "I think," she went on, "that God chose his son to be born like the rest of us so that *we* can realize that we are important."[21]

The woman went on to discuss overcharging in grocery stores and how they would link up with other catechetics groups and base Christian communities around their part of town to organize a boycott of the stores. Base communities turn to political action only on occasion. For the most part these activities would be considered legitimate in a democratic society. Typically they comprise putting pressure on authorities to respond to their demands.

These demands are for basic services, such as mail, water, sewage, schools—services typically found in middle-class neighborhoods. Base communities are a threat to authorities not because violence is likely to erupt but because their demands are put to a system that prefers to keep the poor on the margin of society. Community members seldom have title to the land on which they live. Hence they are not fully enfranchised in the political system.

The Issue of Land Tenure

One of the most threatening of all demands placed on governments by community members is the issue of land. Land tenure holds the key to explaining many of the problems of Latin America and is inextricably woven into the types of disputes that base community members "cause." There are four patterns of conflict over land tenure. First, rural families, as in Brazil, have worked a plot of land for decades or centuries without having to concern themselves with land titles. Their claim can be regarded as undocumented and therefore questionable. When corporations seek large plots of land for mass cultivation, governments eager for agribusiness begin putting these families off the land. In most cases they head for the *favelas* in São Paulo or some other large city. In other cases they resist successfully. In Brazil the church has actively supported the rural poor by means of agrarian leagues, advocacy before the government, or publicizing outrageous situations to larger audiences in order to gain public support. However, the government usually has the upper hand: it is relatively impervious to public opinion (not having been elected) and the site of the conflict is so far away that few justice and peace commissions of church authorities can follow what is going on.

Secondly, some rural families, as in Paraguay, hope to gain title to land by reason of recent colonization projects. A number of them have joined colonization projects through Christian agrarian leagues. The church through the Committee for Rural Pastoral Ministry of the Paraguayan Bishops' Conference and the bishop of Coronel Oviedo attempted to act as agents for the families relocated in colonies. Despite the intervention of the church, there has been harassment by government forces.

Thirdly, some rural families live and work on *latifundia*, huge landed estates, as sharecroppers. Typically they have lived on the same land for decades, in many cases for centuries before the Spanish conquest. Especially in view of the shrinking number of available sites and rising populations, they wish to gain title to the plots they have been working within *latifundia*. Base communities, together with other organizations, have campaigned for this type of land reform. The church has actively promoted land reform and, consistent with its social teaching, has argued the social function of private property. "There is an imperious need for real agrarian and urban reforms," said the bishops at Puebla. "Nor can anyone deny the concentration of power in the hands of civilian and military bureaucracies, which frustrate rightful claims for participation and guarantees in a democratic state."[22] The bishops see clearly the connection between lack of reform and the authoritarian political environment.

Fourthly, forced off the land, rural families migrate to large cities. In places such as Lima or São Paulo recent emigrants periodically gather together and move in on plots of land on the outskirts of the city. They have no other place to claim. They act as squatters, beginning as soon as possible to construct a hovel. Little by little governments have come to accept such invasions or they have created *pueblos jovenes*, "new communities," often at some distance from the inner city. These practices relieve pressures put on the central government by enormous numbers of homeless persons. Squatters, however, find land titles elusive despite government assurances. Base communities get involved in attempts to obtain land titles through barrio associations or through the mediation of their pastors or bishops.

In the four patterns of conflict over land, the church sees merit in the arguments of *campesinos* and slum-dwellers. But governments and the military are ready to put down such arguments as Marxist-inspired. At the very least the base communities and their efforts at land reform are seen as troublesome, indeed dangerous to stability and order. Christian agrarian leagues are closely observed by security forces. Military and paramilitary forces not only monitor their activities but also jail, torture, and cause the disappearance of thousands who have been active in agrarian leagues or land reform efforts. The conflict between the theology of liberation and the ideology of national security is not fought

out on game boards but in the lives of thousands of lay and clerical Christians, many of them members of grassroots Christian
communities. The church is paying a high price to become itself.

Assessment

The Vatican quickly took notice of the rapid spread of base
communities and their potential for bringing disintegration to an
organization that was already structurally weak. After 1972 some
Vatican officials and executives and staff at CELAM headquarters began a closer scrutiny of what was taking place.

In the period before Archbishop Alfonso López Trujillo and
his conservative staff moved into CELAM headquarters in Bogotá in 1972, church leaders regarded base communities as one of
the model embodiments of what the Latin American church had
been struggling to achieve: *pastoral de conjunto,* active involvement of the laity in the church. Such a goal seemed only remotely
attainable in a culture presumed to be ingrained with passivity,
traditionalism, and fatalism. The *comunidades de base* somehow
made pastoral goals come to life. The CELAM conference at
Medellín approved of the existence of the base communities and
hoped that the enterprise would prosper throughout the continent. On their return from the Medellín conference, CELAM
staff set about facilitating the development of base communities
through courses and publications. There was a willingness in
many places to let the groups flourish.

Growth of the communities continued like mushrooms in a rain
forest. But the dangers of uncontrolled growth are evident to anyone who has speculated about or become involved in organizational analysis. The most immediate danger is the potential for
political manipulation and organizational disintegration. Other
dangers are fundamentalism ("enthusiasm without substance" is
one definition), dismantlement of the parish structure (something
that took centuries to establish), and trusteeism (loss of control to
a group of individuals on the local level).

To offset the dangers of political activism among some base
communities, López Trujillo and his CELAM staff sought to give
a spiritualizing interpretation to the concepts of liberation and
church. Key Vatican administrators, such as Archbishop Jerome

Hamer, former subsecretary for the Congregation on Doctrine, favored that line of traditional interpretation. That interpretation did not have to be "forced"; it simply continued the spiritualizing position that traditional Catholic and Protestant biblical scholars took when they interpreted such biblical themes as liberation, poverty, and politics.

By early 1979, with the Puebla conference imminent, the lines of conflict over the base communities were drawn. López Trujillo and others in the Vatican or Latin America thought the base communities should be reined in. Many others took a more moderate stand, arguing only that it was time to scrutinize and evaluate base communities in terms of what they meant for the future of the church.

The Puebla commission dealing with base communities was loaded with Vatican and Latin American conservatives. But the tactic produced embarrassment as draft after draft of the commission was sent back by the plenary group for revision. "The drafts made weak statements about a dynamic reality. They were bound to be rejected by any person who knew what was happening at the grassroots," said Father William Saelman, a Dutch missionary-observer.[23] In the waning days of the conference Bishop Roger Aubry of Bolivia recast the document into a statement about *comunidades eclesiales de base* that proved acceptable to the larger assembly.

So important had the communities become in the bishops' assessment that *comunidades de base* were stressed in several parts of the final document, not only in the section on local church organization. The Puebla assessment of the communities reflects a gain in organizational sophistication over the uncritical praise bestowed at Medellín. The bishops at Puebla recognized base communities as an excellent Latin American adaptation of ideas expressed at Vatican II and as "the hope of the church," but they also acknowledged that the communities could lead to organizational and theological crises. The delegates acknowledged dangers of "organizational anarchy or narrow-minded elitism."[24] The base communities would have to fit in with the larger church if there was to be organizational unity. The danger was recognized without panic. The base communities would go on. But questions of organizational authority remained.

A vexing theological question arose at Puebla from theological formulations or intuitions about community. In the years preceding the Puebla conference the idea of *Iglesia popular* (people's church) had grown in popularity. Proponents of base communities were increasingly promoting the concept of the church as arising from the people. Some proponents would have liked to distance themselves from a historical church that at times embarrassed them with its traditional structures and practices. It took some doing for the unwieldy group of 190 bishops to agree on a statement in which the idea was affirmed but also qualified. Yes, the "church . . . is trying to incarnate itself in the ranks of the common people on our continent, and that therefore arises out of their response in faith to the Lord."[25] But they found the appellation "people's church" unfortunate if it was posed against the institutional church. An important conflict over language was probably avoided, but organizational questions of dispersal and unity, autonomy and centrality, remained.

Enthusiasm for base communities has spread to other parts of the world. When a journalist at Puebla asked Archbishop John Quinn, then president of the U.S. Catholic conference, what key ideas he would take back from the Puebla conference, he said: "Two different issues: multinational corporations and base Christian communities."[26] Within a few months Archbishop Quinn described the issues to U.S. bishops assembled at their semi-annual conference. He received a long ovation.

Some observers doubt the Latin American innovation will export successfully without modification. Even Leo Mahon, one of the pioneers of base communities in Latin America, is not replicating the idea in his new assignment, a large working-class parish in Chicago. "Education is the place to start, not groupings," he reflected.[27] Others disagree. "It is simply too soon to say whether base communities will work on a widespread basis in the U.S.A. or elsewhere," says Rogawski. "We have been helping over ten years to establish base communities in various places in the U.S.A. and I can tell you the idea works among the Spanish-speaking."[28]

In some ways base communities appeal more to Protestants than to Catholics in the U.S.A. References to base communities are now so numerous in Protestant journals that it is no longer necessary to explain what the term means. This is probably because the base community model resembles the historical Protestant model of a congregational church. Professor Peter Kjeseth has said, "The base community vividly updates what we were about before we got into the business of immense suburban church congregations or millions of viewers of the electronic church. Scale of organization and definition of roles will become key issues in the future."[29] The next chapter will further delineate issues of organizational structures and role definitions as the question of the emergence of the laity is gone into.

The Latin American creation of basic Christian communities marks a major achievement. Many of the factors affecting the life of the church in Latin America converge in its genesis: methodologies developed in Catholic Action and liberation theology, pentecostal and Evangelical emphasis on prayer and small communities, the priority of working with the poor promoted by intellectual and pastoral leadership groups, and emphasis on personal commitment and on building up the world stressed by the bishops at Vatican II. The bishops at Puebla saw the communities as "the hope of the future." The communities are ecclesiogenesis, the church being born, the church becoming itself.

5

A New People:
Emergence of the Laity

A tale repeated many times during the debate at Vatican II about the role of the laity in the Church appeared first in skeletal form in the *New Yorker.* An Italian bishop is arguing loudly with colleagues. He sums up his position: "The role of the laity is to pray, pay, and shut up."[1]

By contrast a European observer commenting on emerging lay leadership in the Latin American church wrote: "What is happening is a revolution in the Copernican sense of the term, a complete reversal. A switch [is being made] from a church resting on the point of the pyramid, in the person of bishop or priest, to a church resting upon its base."[2] The implications for changes in authority relationships, role definitions, attainment of status—all core social structures of the church—are enormous. So too are the consequences for politics and society in Latin America.

As important to the Latin American church as are the theology of liberation and the promotion of human rights, they are not the key problem. The crucial issue has received little attention in the *New York Times* or in church journals—publications that tend to focus on the controversies of liberation theology or political activism in the church. The main issue is political—not the worrisome problem of politicization, but internal politics: the emergence of the laity, empowering lay persons for positions of leadership.

The greatest achievement of the Latin American church has been largely ignored: the church is empowering lay persons to a degree and an extent unknown in most other regions of the world. Lay persons are emerging in ways never dreamed possible; they are being empowered for ministry in the church and for secular ministry. They perform functions previously reserved to priests and they are creating new ministries within the church.

They also exercise ministries to society through social service (help to individuals or families) or through social action (activities aimed at making the system more responsive to the needs of "outsiders" or at changing structures). In the case of social action, lay leaders typically begin with a project that addresses an urgent need of the community, such as land distribution, school construction, or water supply. Before long they become aware of the larger realities of national, even transnational, economic and political life. Hence, an internal structural change in the church, empowerment of the laity, has larger social and political implications.

On the basis of reflection on their spiritual and temporal needs, lay persons and their clerical cooperators are creating new lay roles. New roles often match those described in the early Christian communities but present-day invention bases itself on needs and structures of new groups, not on imitation of ancient practice.

Lay leadership in the church is a larger and more complex issue than is the creation of basic Christian communities. The empowerment of the laity for leadership in the Latin American church takes place in many environments other than basic Christian communities. By way of example, the assembly of persons who worship at La Mansión in Santa Cruz, Bolivia, numbers about four thousand—hardly a base community. Lay persons have assumed formally (by invitation) or informally (by initiative) a whole range of roles from liturgical music leadership to teaching groups of several hundred newer members ways to reflect on the Bible and to pray.

Here we focus on the emergence of the laity as it has taken place in base Christian communities only as the most distinct pattern of lay leadership. The chapter examines new authority relationships and their political and social consequences.

Malaise, Threats, and Response

The Catholic Church in Latin America has lacked influence and participation to a degree not often recognized. In most places Latin Americans take part in church worship or social activities to a minor degree. Most Latin Americans receive little formal religious education. Latin American parishes are weak organizationally and in many places they have little impact on the lives of those who live in their neighborhoods. In a word, the Latin American church fails to make contact with the majority of Latin Americans. Exceptions, to be sure, exist—in central Mexico and sections of Colombia and Central America. True, many Latin Americans are emotionally tied to their church. But in terms of participation, knowledge, and ethics, Catholicism is the religion of a minority.

Lack of Latin American clergymen exacerbates the weakness of the church. The scarcity of priests is due partially to assassinations, laicization of former priests, and return home of expatriate missionaries. In addition, the number of new priests is not keeping up with population increases.

The presence of many clergymen from other countries creates other problems. Their presence brings with it cultural shock for the receiving church and often creates confusion in the minds of many Latin Americans. These confusions add to the flux and insecurity created by Vatican II and to further confusion caused by political upheavals in a number of Latin American societies. (Brazilian and Chilean Catholics, to name only more prominent cases, found themselves reeling from the impact of political and religious insecurities.) In this context, foreign priests could not provide for the personal and organizational needs of Latin American Catholics on a permanent basis.

Further, Protestant sects and naturalistic religious cults have made great inroads in many Latin American countries. Whereas historical Protestant churches have ministered to immigrant German- or English-speaking populations or have attracted some middle-class former Catholics, groups such as the Seventh Day

Adventists, Mormons, and, above all, Evangelicals have attracted large masses of rural and urban poor, especially in Chile, Brazil, and Guatemala. Large numbers of Latin Americans practice spiritism, imported from Africa or native to the region. Many Amerindians of the highland Andes or Guatemala continue the naturalistic religions of their forebears, often with an overlay of Catholicism.

All in all, as Bruneau points out, for every Catholic actively practicing his or her religion, in many countries an equal or larger number of Latin Americans participate in some other form of religion.[3] This occurs especially "at the base" of the population. The poor and the working class were not abandoned by the church; many priests and sisters heroically attended to them. But the lower classes were not given attention proportionate to their numbers, especially in basic evangelization or education. The church perceived increasingly that its potential base was being eroded by Protestant inroads and by the practice of spiritism or other naturalistic religions.

In the middle class, competition for loyalty came from the secular left. The previous challenge of Masonic free thought or liberalism gave way to threats posed by socialism or various forms of communism. Universities, especially large, urban universities, became the battleground for conflicting ideologies. To meet challenges to the loyalties of the middle class, the Latin American church turned to imported—or in a very few cases self-initiated—strategies. They proved largely transitory and ineffective.

To meet these external threats the church had to employ lay leaders. Not only were there not enough priests but priests would not be accepted in secular circles in the same way that lay persons are.

In the larger church the issue became known as "the problem of the laity." Intellectuals, primarily articulate lay persons in Europe and the U.S.A. and European theologians, began facing the problem of the legitimation and promotion of the laity. Many lay persons, especially the more educated, wanted a more active role in the church. What place should they have in the church?

Church strategists were also aware of the pastoral challenge represented by largely passive masses of baptized Catholics in Europe. In contemporary life persons belonging to an organization with little intellectual or emotional involvement were likely to drift away from the institution, as many of the working class did in France and Italy. Moreover, serious external threats arose first from Protestants, then from anti-Catholics in revolutionary governments, and finally from communists and old-line socialists. Leaders within the church, such as Canon Joseph Cardijn and Father Adolph Kolping, created movements and structures to meet challenges to the loyalties of the middle and working classes as well as to meet demands for more active participation in the church by the laity. Thus a number of lay movements began in Europe.

What became painfully obvious was that there was no ideology sufficient to back up the movements: a theology of the laity (and hence an amplified theology of the church) was needed. Various factors began influencing the genesis and direction of this ideology. First, the incongruence of masses of inactive Catholics in democratic countries where participation was expected became increasingly evident. Secondly, Protestant churches had already reformed the ideology, if not fully the reality, of lay participation. As Catholics and Protestants increased their interaction, especially in northern Europe and the United States, the Protestant model exerted an influence on Catholics, clerical and lay. Finally, theological, biblical, patristic, and liturgical movements all pointed to the necessity of active involvement of the laity in the church. Historical and systematic scholarship began drawing the main outlines of a theology of the laity. Major theologians such as Congar and Rahner were attracted to the question because of their concern to rethink the nature of the church.[4] And the laity was demanding an adequate intellectual conception of its role. It was no accident that many theologians confronting the problem worked closely with worker-priests or directly with lay persons.

What place was the laity to occupy in the church? Focus on the term "laity" led nowhere. The laity consisted of nonclerics and nonmembers of religious congregations. They were called the faithful or parishioners, terms without much meaning in the modern era. Instead, theologians focused directly on what it meant to be a Christian in the world: the theology of the laity developed within the context of an evolving theology of the church at the service of the world.

Congar, Rahner, and others focused on and elaborated the central concept of the priesthood of the faithful, based on recent research into biblical and early church sources. Vatican II absorbed and diffused their formulations of the church and the place of the laity within the church. An ideology sufficient for the emergence of the laity had been created; lay persons had gained legitimacy for assuming active roles in the church.

Lay Typologies

As the history of the Latin American church has unfolded, several distinct types of laity have appeared. Because of their differing basic orientations, their relationship with the formal church differs as also the nature and relative strength of demands they can make. As the laity emerge in the church, it wields power and gains status in new ways. It is presumed but not proven that an evolution of the laity through various types is taking place within the church. The description offered here is not meant to be definitive but suggestive of what one finds when viewing the church from the grass roots.

Traditional Catholics

Traditional Catholics are the millions who are members of the church by reason of culture and family. In Latin America the vast majority think of themselves as *católico,* whether or not they participate in church activities and whether or not they earnestly follow Christian mandates. They are born into a society that is Catholic. The distinction between church and world that Catholic Action wished to make was virtually unintelligible to them. Their world is Catholic; how could it be otherwise?

Thus a married man might have "affairs" with various women and almost never attend church but continue to consider himself *católico,* although not *muy católico.* God is merciful, and upon proper repentance and reform one could return to the full sense of being Catholic. He would cease being Catholic only by a deliberate act of renunciation. Even joining a fundamentalist evangelical sect is not always seen as a repudiation of Catholic identity.

Traditional Catholics are noted for their passivity. The laity for the most part watches in silence as ceremonies are performed for it by a priest with some minimal lay assistance in the form of altar servers, sacristans, ushers, or choir members. Decisions about building or financing are taken unilaterally by pastors, sometimes in consultation with monied elites. Catholic education is largely a passive experience and reaches only a minority of Catholics, usually, but not exclusively, from the middle and upper classes.

In the traditional church, preaching, preparation for sacraments, visiting the sick and elderly, and deciding what political positions the church should take are all in the hands of priests and bishops. Parish life is organizationally weak, as is its hold over the emotional involvement of the laity. The vastness of parishes, many embracing tens of thousands of members, accounts in part for the psychological distance between laity and clergy. Lay persons lament their inability to find a community spirit in the large groupings of parishioners from different neighborhoods and often from differing class backgrounds. Nor can they find comfortable solidarity with their social superiors—much less with their oppressors.

Moreover, the Latin American laity identifies its church more closely with the bishop than with the pastor. Lay persons may not know their pastor's name; they are more likely to know the name of their bishop and express more interest in him and his welfare. This identification derives from the weakness of parish structures, from the social status of the bishop (estimated as roughly equivalent to that of mayor or provincial governor), and from the Latin American cultural emphasis on the role of *patrones,* especially regional *patrones.* Finally, power, real power, resides in the bishops. They can "make or break" pastors and they represent the church before civil power to a degree that priests do not. In brief, in the traditional church, decentralized and organizationally weak, the episcopacy is the primary seat of power. Such empowerment derives from a traditionally understood biblical precedent for the role of the bishop, reinforced by a medieval variant that made the bishop parallel to a regional prince or lord.

Transitional Types

New lay movements began to emerge in the church in the 1920s and '30s. This development gradually gained momentum and strength by the time of Vatican II. With the ideology of a renewed church that included an active role for the laity, Vatican II opened new doors. Two years after the council, in an unpublished study, Vallier identified three types of new lay leaders in Chile. Roughly the same types were emerging in other Latin American countries.

One of the distinctive lay leadership types is that of the technicians and professionals directly working for the church or for one of its loosely affiliated organizations. These men and women work in institutes such as the Centro Bellarmino, or in relief agencies such as Caritas/Catholic Relief, or in a variety of new church programs such as radio schools, cooperatives, or human rights organizations. Salaries come directly from bishops or from overseas funding. These persons are employed in an organizational system that is Christian, increasingly ecumenical, enterprising, and managerial. They are hired to provide technical knowledge in some specialized area.

Final authority resides typically in the hands of the priests who act as directors or implicitly as "chairmen of the board." Although lay persons wish autonomy by reason of their expertise, they find goals, workloads, and use of technical data constrained from above.

A second and much more common type of lay leaders is that of the men and women who help manage, lead, and develop the church's apostolic movements and lay organizations. They include groups such as Catholic Action and the *Cursillos de Cristiandad*, which had national impact, as well as the Jesuit Sodality and the Legion of Mary, whose influence was local and low-keyed. Almost all leaders in these organizations work on a volunteer basis. Members contribute a large part of the money and time needed for programs, with additional funds coming from bishops or more frequently from overseas (including the CIA and German bishops, interested in combating communism). A few salaried leaders can be found at the diocesan or national level.

Lay leaders in these organizations concentrate their programs on building and renewing motivational commitments of lay Catholics and then giving these energies some focus in terms of "good works" or useful projects. They are joiners and they want other lay persons to recognize the importance of their groups and to be involved in them. These lay leaders come from middle-class backgrounds with a few members from the working class or the upper class. Their occupations vary from professional (lawyers, engineers, teachers) to middle-management, small business owners, and housewives. Older members (those in their fifties or beyond) tend to have as their institutional frame of reference the local or diocesan level. By contrast many student members and young professionals focus on the provincial and national levels. Many have taken the next logical step and helped found national political parties, such as Popular Action in Brazil or Christian Democracy in Chile, Bolivia, and elsewhere.

The main point of contact with the clergy is not so much with pastors of local parishes as with chaplains of these movements and organizations. Their work gives them recognition, social status, and close affiliation with the clergy. Many leaders have been deeply involved for a long time in lay organizations: youth movements, educational programs, apostolic movements, or diocesan councils.

A third type of lay leader is that of independent Catholics who are also prominent members of society. They are doctors, corporation executives, political and governmental officials, university professors, and prosperous lawyers. They gained their positions in secular society on the basis of professional performance, inherited wealth, or political popularity. They are not linked to the church in terms of their professional skills; they are occupationally independent. But they are highly committed Catholics, closely attuned to the policies and activities of church leadership groups. Their main contacts with the church are through liturgical and sacramental services.

These lay leaders often have priests as close friends. They are the integrators of Catholic and secular culture; they are daily involved in the financial and power centers of society and they experience the pressures and pulls that these involvements generate. They vary in their political propensities, from the highly liberal or progressive professional, to the conservative business type who, often enough, has ties with the landed groups in the country.

These men and women do not work routinely under clerical supervision nor do they work as collaborators with priests in specialized fields, nor do they rely heavily on their services as chaplains. Removed from the work-a-day world of the institutional church and relatively uninvolved in conventional lay organizations, they naturally view the clergy in terms of different frameworks and make different kinds of demands on the clergy. Their principal referrants are bishops, not priests, and they express their opinions in ways that indicate their capacities to see the "larger picture."

Postconciliar Laity in Base Communities

Emphasis shifted in the Latin American church from joining traditional lay organizations to focusing energies and resources on grassroots Christian communities. These efforts are by no means universal but they are spurred by the new ideology and pastoral strategy enunciated by the church at the Medellín and Puebla conferences. Base Christian communities became the preferred but not exclusive pastoral strategy of the progressive leadership groups in the church.

An evolution has taken place in the efforts of the church to empower the laity. As Vatican II unfolded a new theology of the church in the world and a new ideology of inclusion and empowerment of the laity, Latin American pastoral leaders began a continentwide discussion of how this inclusion and empowerment might take place. Initial efforts were uncertain in detail and unclear in definition. In a general way inclusion of the laity in church activities and its empowerment for certain roles was described as *pastoral de conjunto* (joint pastoral ministry). This term remained plastic, applicable to myriad structures and roles. In short, *pastoral de conjunto* stood for "somehow let's involve the laity."

Pastoral de conjunto began evolving into *comunidades de base* in a number of distinct locations: Brazil, Chile, Paraguay, the Dominican Republic, and Central America. Several factors were responsible for their creation and expansion (some have already been alluded to above); not all factors were operative in every location. The single most universal factor within the church was the driving force of progressives who wished to emphasize social justice. This, as we have seen, meant siding with the poor and working directly and extensively with them. Moreover there was a recognition throughout Latin America that no institution, whether political, social, or religious, would succeed without involvement at the base. Finally, the pentecostal sects and naturalistic religions set an example of how to work successfully at the grassroots. Most base communities have emerged in repressive political environments. The social control exercised by these regimes—restriction on speaking in the public forum—meant that the only "safe" place was with the people, relatively out of sight. These factors are diagramed in Figure 1.

Figure 1
Development of *Comunidades de Base*
in Repressive Environments

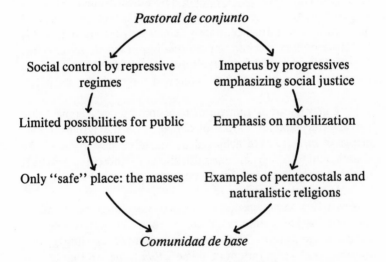

Pastoral de conjunto

Social control by repressive regimes

Impetus by progressives emphasizing social justice

Limited possibilities for public exposure

Emphasis on mobilization

Only "safe" place: the masses

Examples of pentecostals and naturalistic religions

Comunidad de base

Base Christian communities have become a revitalization movement for laity and clergy alike. For individual members the community has brought about a religious experience. The community also fostered consecration, commitment. Life in the community brought with it a whole new perception of what it meant to be a Christian. Ultimately commitment to a base community meant fulfillment of Christian life for community members.

Association, Status, and Power

From a sociological perspective the base community experience brings with it a new relationship to the church. Church members shift from a parochial to an associational relationship to the church. They make a deliberate choice to be a Catholic. This commitment is often missing in simply belonging to a Catholic society, but it is inherent in membership in a base community. That someone would continue to commit grave injustices while still belonging to a base community is repugnant to community members; sooner or later the offender will drop out of the base community.

In terms of status another major shift occurs for base community members. Status as a Catholic is no longer "inherited"; it is achieved. Inherited status comes from one's family, is beyond one's control or influence, unless deliberately renounced, and is therefore neither merited nor especially rewarded. By contrast achieved status results from one's own efforts, can be lost if these efforts are not continued, and is merited and rewarded in special ways.

With new status attainment as base community members, lay persons can make new types of demands on the system. Other increases in status are achieved by fulfilling new roles in the church; and fulfilling new roles also allows for increased demands on the church. In a word, enhanced status has brought new power to the laity in the church.

Newspaper and magazine accounts of the church often reflect assumptions commonly made about power in the church as a formal organization. The church is portrayed as similar to a transnational corporation or some other type of tightly-knit bureaucracy—less tightly organized than an army but more than a hospital bureaucracy. Power is assumed to reside at the top, filtering down from pope, Vatican inner circles, and local bishops to local pastors. By the time power reaches the grassroots, it is insignificant or more symbolic than factual: reading liturgical texts or presenting liturgical offerings.

Such a conception overlooks the associational aspect of the

church evolving in Latin America. The base Christian community is an association "owned" by its members, each of whom possesses a portion of power. Many members of base communities have extensive and direct power. They can support or oppose the person or policies of bishop or pastor. They can attend or stay away from meetings. They can volunteer or refuse to serve. They can contribute or withhold financial resources. They exercise ultimate power by withdrawing their personal involvement.

Church officials act as power brokers as well as authorities. Pastors and bishops collect power from individuals and channel it into programs and functions that lay persons will not withdraw their power from. The fact that power also arises from the base considerably modifies the assumptions of those who have pictured the church as roughly equivalent to Exxon. The bottom-up view also helps to explain the power dynamics of the grassroots communities and new roles fashioned for and by lay men and women.

Some measure of bureaucracy will always be maintained in the church. A transnational agency in the contemporary world could not exist or function effectively without some formal authority, control, and lines of communication. Moreover church superiors have sources of power not typically available to leaders of wholly voluntary associations. By office, bishops are guardians of long-standing traditions—that is, established ways to believe, worship, and practice. In part, they control the symbols and myths of the organization.

But the bishops control only in part. Not only do they need volunteers but typically they themselves are not professional scholars in the areas of belief, worship, or practice. Another group completes the triangle. Biblical exegetes, patristic scholars, systematic theologians, liturgical experts, and moral theologians are needed to examine symbols, myths, and ideology systematically. These three groups—superiors, experts, and laity—have been in interaction for centuries. Wielding of influence and making of policy is thus a multifaceted enterprise, with influence in the church being exercised at one time or another by each of the three groups. Interchange is usually cooperative but conflicts arise periodically on a variety of issues, such as the Hans Küng controversy or the widespread nonacceptance of birth-control restrictions. Potential for tension and conflict between the three groups is an ever-present factor in the life of the church.

Structural Changes in the Local Church

Structural changes refer here to the way the local church is organized, the way power is exercised, and the availability and type of rewards for participants. The traditional local church was noted, first, for a pastor who held centralized, diffuse power—that is, he made decisions over many areas (finances, administration, education, and worship) without necessarily having expertise in each area. Secondly, parishes, and the church generally in Latin America, lacked accountability structures. In many places the church was so loosely organized and decentralized that pastors did pretty much as they wished and seldom had to make an account to parish members or superiors. This was true, too, of priests working in educational, relief, or social action agencies. Bishops typically stepped in to ask for accountability only under pressure from outside sources. Thirdly, the traditional church, by and large, lacked meaningful rewards for grassroots members. Achieved status (by reason of belonging to a respected lay organization) or positional status (by reason of a role played) was available to the middle class. But for those at the grassroots, the rural and urban poor, such rewards were unavailable in most places.

The new church, as exemplified by the base communities, has made crucial structural changes that affect the life of the laity:

1. *Scale of community*. The virtual impossibility of developing full organizational life and a sense of identity among thousands of persons in an urban or rural parish is avoided by the size of the base communities. The reduction in size to, say, twelve to twenty couples allows participants to "own" the group by sharing power and helping to make decisions, by speaking up and being heard, and by being held accountable.

2. *Homogeneous groups*. As a rule those who belong to base communities come from the same small village or urban subneighborhood. Not only are the members neighbors but they usually have the same economic background and subculture, typically *campesino* or working class. Base communities are group-

ings of neighbors who become involved with one another and become committed to the biblical Christ and the larger church. (Considerable difficulties loom for the larger church as a result of the homogeneity and encapsulation of some base communities, engendering, ironically, "parochial" views.)

3. *Diffusion of power and division of labor.* In the new church the priest shares power with the laity. Lay persons preside over or participate actively in worship, they teach new members, they make decisions about their lives (no longer dichotomized into spiritual and temporal spheres), and they minister to the sick or foster projects such as the digging of a well, the construction of a road, or the obtaining of land titles.

4. *Accountability structures.* The lack of accountability structures that marks the traditional Latin American church is not generally to be found in the new communities. Members are held accountable to other members for conduct inside and outside the group. Group membership entails acceptance of group norms; in this case members are presumed to be attempting to live up to a general understanding of the Ten Commandments. Grave or continued deviance is met by challenge, ostracization, or expulsion.

Base community members make demands on the services of the pastor or bishop through group presidents or coordinators. Likewise the priest or bishop can challenge the group to new growth or activities or, through lay moderators, can hold it accountable for dubious activities. Accountability of the small groups is not sought typically for authoritarian ends but rather to harness the resources of the laity toward the corporate goals of the larger church.

5. *Meaningful status rewards.* The church, traditional or revitalized, offers members considerable rewards, such as the promise of ultimate deliverance (if they are faithful) and certitude of basic religious beliefs. These rewards may suffice for some self-motivated individuals but most grassroots members need rewards of higher status to become more actively involved in the life of the institution. Providing such rewards is a central concern for any organization that must enlist volunteers. (Voluntary organizations in the U.S.A., such as candy-stripers in hospitals or Boy Scouts, are especially adept at attracting participants through symbols and activities such as costumes, titles, and functions that

are perceived to be worthwhile.) The base community bestows achieved status on members upon entrance into the group and adherence to its norms. They gain further status through acceptance and performance of roles within the group.

6. *Legitimation and formalization of lay roles*. Although the group decides or helps to decide who will exercise certain functions within it, the pastor or bishop typically installs new office holders in a formal ceremony. As lay leadership emerged, legitimation became a key issue. Despite the bishop's or priest's acceptance of lay persons for roles within the church, reaction occurred in some places against accepting what were believed to be priestly functions from persons who were not priests. Accordingly bishops and priests composed ceremonies of lay ministerial legitimation that were like ordinations. In some cases it was necessary for lay ministers sent to other communities to have papers signed and sealed by the bishop, stating that they were empowered as minister of baptism, of communion, or whatever new function they were to perform. New ceremonies of office conferral tend to be simple; they usually take place in a group prayer meeting or during the parish liturgy. In some places, such as Santiago de los Caballeros (Dominican Republic), assumption of the role of *presidente* of a community is treated as a weighty responsibility: bestowal of full title is very formal and is granted only after an apprenticeship.

7. *Training and socialization*. From an organizational perspective the weakest aspect of the new communities has been the lack of training for some of the new roles. Some functions are simple in scope and require no special training. Some leadership roles can be performed by persons who already know how to animate a group toward some goal. The communities also enlist those with previous training, such as school teachers. Nonetheless, school teachers and other community members have only a sketchy awareness of the history and content of the Bible and derived theological formulations. This vulnerability has been recognized in many places; dioceses have established permanent centers for training leaders.

The efforts of the church to select and train lay leaders have resulted in a massive shift in church personnel away from the middle and upper classes. A major force in the Latin American church, the Latin American Conference of Religious (priests, brothers, and sisters who are members of religious congregations), estimates that about 60 percent of its members are working with urban or rural poor, in many instances as teachers or catalysts of self-help programs.[5]

Lay Persons and Ministers

Military and other security forces closely monitored the progress and activities of lay persons who were members of base communities. The Vatican and CELAM, too, sensed dangers and problems. Questions were raised at times about the teachings proposed by one or another base community. However, the main concern of higher officials was not doctrinal but organizational. From this point of view the base Christian communities offered many potential headaches, seemingly more than the Latin American church could bear. Could an already organizationally weak institution absorb more decentralization? Would diffusion of power from the center to the peripheries—the sharing of the power of priest and bishop—mean potential disintegration? What would happen to the unity essential to any organization?

Vatican officials, perceiving the threats, flocked to the Puebla meeting. Pope John Paul's central message at Puebla was a plea for unity, seeking a base from which to begin his potentially long-term papacy.[6] As chief executive of an extensive transnational organization, he saw some ominous implications in the emergence of grassroots communities and of subsequent structural changes in the Latin American church. No president of General Motors would have acceded to a corresponding decentralization of functions and power within his corporation. Similarly no army general views extensive decentralization as the pattern for modern armies. Nonetheless John Paul and the Vatican approved the Latin American mandate for base communities and the emergence of the laity that it implied.

A major reason why the community movement was approved and in many places is actively encouraged is that the demands of the laity in these communities are basically religious. For the most part community members are seeking enlightenment, spiritual growth, and the improvement of their human condition. Few lay persons in Latin America are demanding "citizen's rights," such as "one person, one vote." Moreover, where lay persons are emerging in the church they do so typically in an atmosphere of mutual trust between laity and clergy. Further, lay persons in these communities want to remain Roman Catholics; they are not seeking some other kind of church.

Finally, fifteen years of experience with base communities have shown researchers that the communities almost always continue to exist only where priests or religious sisters actively promote them.[7] Similar to the Protestant experience in the U.S.A., the pastor is largely responsible for creating the kind of climate in which volunteer workers flourish.[8] Without the pastor's blessing and active encouragement, lay groups tend to fade away.

The potential organizational threats posed by the base communities thus have failed to materialize. Moreover, from a positive point of view, the grassroots communities and the emergence of the laity correspond to a basic change in outlook in the worldwide church expressed at Vatican II. Finally lay emergence and base communities reflect the global hierarchy's growing appreciation of the needs and aspirations of the rank and file.

Unresolved Issues

The emergence of the laity unlocks a whole series of questions, too complex and inchoate to discuss here beyond merely outlining major questions. First, an active place for the laity means an adjustment in the role of the priest. Indeed a "new" priest is emerging along with the new laity.[9] He devotes more of his time to religious functions and less time to administrative and financial work. He needs time to keep up with the new religious ideology of the church and to follow research in biblical and theological fields. He concentrates more on his own spiritual development as well as that of his lay collaborators. Homilies are much more demanding now that his listeners are reading the Bible and seeking to make their own interpretations of what they read and what they experience in life. Some outlines of the new priesthood are thus being drawn. Whether that kind of priest can be fashioned in a traditional seminary setting is still another question.

Given the heightened activity of lay men and women in the

Latin American church, observers from the U.S.A. and Europe invariably raise the question of the ordination of women or at least of the bestowal of greater status. The Latin American church will probably work out those questions differently from the churches in the United States and Europe, given the cultural differences. Not only are women "starting from further back" in some ways, but the ways in which cultural and political conflicts are resolved in Latin America differ from Anglo-Saxon ways.

A great lacuna in the first formulations of liberation theology was that of the role of women in Latin American culture and in the church. Theologians soon found themselves challenged on this point, especially in international conferences and in confrontations with women activists in Latin America. Latin American bishops also have been challenged on the issue. The result has been an increasing sensitivity to the problem. Archbishop Marcos McGrath, chairman of the central steering committee at Puebla, observed that the church had only recently opened its consciousness to the problem, that advances had been made (as witnessed by the presence of women delegates and observers at that very conference), and that further progress would be made.[10] Clearly changes at the hierarchical level would proceed at an evolutionary—not a precipitous—pace.

At the local level, something of a revolution has already taken place in practice, if not in ideology. The Latin American church has been less fussy about distinctions of lay-clerical status and functions than has the church in the U.S.A. In Brazil and elsewhere women are performing many functions (preaching, baptizing, giving communion) previously reserved to priests. Priests and bishops in Latin America have had the opportunity to note the effective work of women in such capacities. In a sense, then, some women in Latin America have made greater inroads than have most women in U.S. churches, Catholic or Protestant. The power of women in the Latin American church grows from practice.

The place of women in Latin American culture and in the church evidences some further subtleties, none more important than the question of how decisions are made.[11] To allow macho cultural stereotypes to suggest that Latin American women are relegated to the margins of effective participation in society and in the church is to overlook the residual power of women in Latin America. A glimpse of this extensive phenomenon is provided by considering what takes place in a base community: decisions are made with the active contribution of women, many of whom act as leaders in the group; often women are the chief decision-makers.

The ordination of women is not a high priority among Latin American bishops. But many of them have spoken in favor of a married priesthood. Latin American bishops have been leaders in bringing forward this question during various synods in Rome after Vatican II and many bishops discuss the issue directly with Pope John Paul in their official *ad limina* (quinquennial) visits to Rome.

Biblical scholars and theologians agree generally that there is no compelling theological argument against a married priesthood. Many Latin American bishops find compelling organizational reasons for married priests. Five hundred years of a celibate priesthood have left a greatly reduced priest-to-population ratio. Nor can a national church continue indefinitely to import foreign clergymen. Even more critical, among some cultures, such as that of Andean Amerindians, the concept of unmarried, childless priests is not well understood or accepted. How soon a married clergy will be allowed in the church remains to be seen, but when it happens it will probably occur first in Latin America—a further indication of the leadership of the Latin American church.

When celibacy becomes optional, the first step will probably be the reincorporation of many who left the priesthood and got married. Many of these men would like to function as priests and have so petitioned the bishops. Furthermore, large numbers of lay men are already prepared to assume the priesthood. They have been catechists for periods of ten to twenty years, have a solid commitment to the church, and could assume the full role of the priesthood with little additional training. Many of these men are recognized as leaders within their communities and could more easily and effectively exercise the priestly office than can missionaries who remain outsiders by reason of culture or nationality.

In sum, influential leaders in the Latin American church have moved the institution on a progressive course. These leaders have relied on experts to provide new ideology and directions for the church. The new ideology brought the laity much greater prominence. It was an evolutionary process: the church did not immediately or completely empower lay men and women but it opened the door to new role definitions and conferred new status and power on the laity. The social background of the newest lay leaders represents another change. The men and women standing center stage in the 1980s are rural and urban poor. They have upstaged the educated and middle class.

The emergence of the laity represents the greatest achievement of the Latin American church. The movement is not complete but it is underway in the base communities. The result has been a release of resources and energy only hinted at in the days before Vatican II. Structural changes in the local church have taken place as a result of the movement. Power is now shared, accountability structures have appeared, and status rewards are offered the rank and file. "We are," remarked a leading Latin American bishop, "setting free the people of God to serve him."[12] A Copernican revolution is taking place in the Latin American church.

6

A New Political Environment:
The Church and the Military
in Conflict

Leonidas Proaño, one of the best known Latin American bishops, invited some church leaders whose friendship he had made during and after Vatican II to his home in Riobamba, Ecuador. There seventeen bishops, including four from the United States, and twenty-nine priests, sisters, and lay persons, were to reflect on the current state of affairs in the church.[1]

On the second day of the meeting, men dressed as civilians, carrying pistols and automatic weapons, entered the house. For the most part, they were silent, refusing to speak; they offered no identification and gave no explanation. Then they manhandled two of the bishops and took all forty-six participants to Quito and jail.

After a day of confinement all were let go or were sent out of the country, except for Proaño who was questioned through the night and held for another twenty-four hours. His questioners were agents of the military regime. The issue at stake was a working document of the Center for Nonviolence with which Proaño was associated. This harassment, involving one of the most prominent progressive bishops in Latin America, was meant to stifle

146

criticism of the social order under military rule. The subsequent smear campaign and the manhandling of Chilean delegates at the Santiago airport by secret police were signs of a regional military conspiracy.

The break-in and the jailing of the bishops illustrate a tense and tortuous church-military relationship as it has existed in much of Latin America. A change in the relationship began taking place when the military as an institution took over rule in one Latin American country after another. As Penny Lernoux points out, "Nelson Rockefeller in 1969 was one of the first to predict that the military and the church would be the principal actors in Latin America's coming political drama."[2]

Why is the church, a religious institution, concerned with the political environment? As a major institution in society the church has to act in the political arena. The church achieves its corporate goals in a social environment that in large part is governed by the rules of the political order.

Before Vatican II churchmen considered most of the goals of the church to be internal, realizable within the confines of the church. Its major goals—praise of God, sanctification of members through prayer and sacraments, and education in the gospel message—could be achieved internally. Twenty years ago the only major goal that was overtly political was organization-maintenance. And at times national churches spent vast amounts of energy to maintain the organization, given a political environment of antichurch liberals or populist revolutionaries.

Since Vatican II and the Medellín and Puebla conferences, the self-understanding of the church has changed. The church created a "new" ideology for itself. This ideology holds that goals of the church that were to be accomplished internally are now to be achieved externally as well. Praise of God, sanctification of members, and communication of the gospel message are all to be oriented to activity in society. In a word, church leaders and their ideologues began changing an otherworldly religion to a this-worldly religion, with at least indirect political consequences.

The deaths of dozens of priests and sisters and thousands of lay persons at the hands of military and security forces leave many questions. Why is the military frequently in conflict with the church? What in the military character allows some officers to look upon the church as an enemy and ranking clerics, such as Dom Hélder Câmara, as communist "plants?" What moves the military in El Salvador and many other countries to employ paramilitary as death squads?

The Changing Political Scene

Until recently, more than half the population of Latin America has lived under military rule. No longer was it a *caudillo* who took over the government and controlled it personalistically but a whole institution that took command of the regime. This was a major shift from the days of Fulgencio Batista in Cuba, Marcos Pérez Jiménez in Venezuela, or the Somoza dynasty in Nicaragua. The change occurred largely since 1964.

The government in many Latin American countries became in part a military institution. Even where the military did not occupy the presidential chair, it was usually a considerable force in the governing elite. The size and strength of the military, its virtual monopoly of force, enhanced its sharing of power. As a large corporate body, the military established new game rules in the conduct of national life. This corporate aspect is seldom considered. But corporate features—hierarchy of command, impersonal quality of military behavior, and diffuseness of responsibility— had profound consequences for those attempting political activity or social reform.

The military also developed an ideology that purported to explain social, economic, and political reality. This is the doctrine of national security. The church, for one, actively opposed that doctrine.

The military has given up the personalistic politics of the *caudillo* general. That type of politics is disdained as unprofessional. Instead, military regimes have tended to rule from institutional authoritarian platforms, having consequences for all who enter the political sphere.

The focus here will be on the South American situation. The discussion has relevance for Central America and the Caribbean, but these subregions will not be taken up directly. Employed will be middle-level analysis based on recent country-by-country studies and interviews conducted from 1964 to 1984.[3] The year

1964 is an appropriate entry point for the discussion because "permanent" military rule began that year in Brazil, marking a new order of things in Latin America. Similar military takeovers would be taking place soon in neighboring countries. For its part, the Catholic Church concluded the Second Vatican Council in 1965, also marking the beginning of a new era.

One by one, South American countries came under military rule. First Brazil and Bolivia in 1964, then Argentina, Peru, Chile, Uruguay, and Ecuador. Centering the lower triangle was General Stroessner and the Paraguayan military who had been in power as long as anyone could recall. All but the northern perimeter with Colombia and Venezuela were run directly by the armed forces.

In Colombia and Venezuela, too, the army at times has acted as a shadow government. During the 1950s and '60s in Venezuela and at least since 1960 in Colombia, the army has monitored critics of the government, dissolved or controlled labor unions and universities, and conducted a general overview of political activities. Amnesty International reported in 1980 that the Colombian army maintained thirty-three prisons or detention centers where political activists were held. In a sense, Colombia has been in a state of seige for more than twenty years, maintained largely by the army and national police. Security forces maintain a highly visible, extensive, and dominant presence. In daytime one sees soldiers alone or in pairs patrolling with rifles or automatic weapons in many districts of Bogotá; at night one finds a soldier or policeman on every block or two in more fashionable sections such as Chapinero.

In countries not directly run by the military, the physical and psychological presence of the army is felt by those who play the political game or who have attempted even episodic political action. The army lays down the rules of the game or enforces the limits beyond which one may not go. This has been true throughout much of the contemporary history of the "democratic" Dominican Republic and Venezuela. In the Dominican Republic the army routinely breaks up strikes of sugarcane workers, blocks unionization efforts, and monitors certain political parties and university political activity.

This chapter will first point out three key themes that permeate

the political environment. Then it will enlarge upon concrete issues in church-military relationships, specific aspects of the new
political environment of the church. This will lead to an examination of the changing stance of the church and of the armed forces
in politics.

The first of the three major themes of this chapter is that the
church has not and does not fully comprehend the nature of its
new political environment. Having made dramatic changes at the
Medellín conference, it did not consider systematically what the
changes would mean to other political bodies. The new self-
understanding of itself as a "servant church" and a church that
would give preferential treatment to the poor would have enormous consequences in the political order.

Because the Latin American church did not think of itself as a
regular (and important) political factor, it did not reflect on the
political effects that would result from its changes. Rather the
church (encouraged by Rome) thought of itself as above, or at
least outside, politics. If ever it had to act politically, it would be
on an episodic basis. Thus, the church ignored, at least at the
beginning of this period, the effects on its political environment
of the changes it proposed for itself. It also ignored for a long time
changes taking place in its former political ally, the armed forces.

The second theme running throughout this chapter is that, inasmuch as the church only partially understood the political environment with which it was dealing, its own political responses
have often been inadequate. Further, its actions have often been
misunderstood as inappropriate, out of step with what had already been decided by authoritarian governments. The military
became impatient with the "meddling" of the church—its prophetic criticism of authoritarian tactics—or enraged at questions
of legitimacy or corruption. The extent of this impatience and
rage is seen in the deaths, disappearances, imprisonments, and
banishments that the church has had to endure.

The third theme is one that has already been developed: the
church is counteracting authoritarian regimes in the best possible
way: it is building grassroots communities, thereby preparing the
masses for participation in national life. This counteracts the ten-

dency of military governments to do away with or severely curtail popular participation.

Conflict Issues

In the years since the first military takeover and the beginning of "permanent" military rule in 1964, conflicts that the church has had with the military have arisen especially over four issues: specific military practices, military doctrine, the goals of military rule, and the consequences of military rule.

Specific Military Practices

The first type of conflict has to do with specific military policies, especially when the military is in power. But this conflict also exists in countries where the military has not ruled directly for a number of years—for example, Colombia. The church has long criticized indiscriminate repression, torture, censorship, and denial of *habeas corpus*. These are human rights in the narrower sense. But the church has also consistently criticized the military for the lack of extensive and free participation in the political and social life of a country. These are human rights in a larger sense, a topic not emphasized even by President Jimmy Carter's overseas human rights campaign.

When the military seized power in eight of the ten South American countries beginning in the mid-1960s, the correlation of military intervention and social conflict became most notable in the southern tier countries—Argentina, Bolivia, Brazil, Chile, and Paraguay. These regimes systematically violated a whole range of human rights. Priests, sisters, and lay persons have been killed, expelled, imprisoned, or have disappeared in notable numbers.[4] Violations of human rights in the larger sense will be considered in the fourth area of conflict.

What was happening in those five southern tier countries mirrored what was happening in a number of other countries, though usually in an intermittent or milder manner—with the conspicuous exception of El Salvador, Guatemala, and Nicaragua under the Somozas. Also notable in those five countries was the organized way that the church has attempted to fight back, even though at the time it did not fully comprehend the "enemy" it was fighting.

At the beginning, in 1964, conflict over human rights was relatively mild. By 1969 the situation had grown much more serious. In that year popular magazines reported that torture was now systematic in Latin America. The five years between 1964 and 1969 were to witness a much greater involvement on the part of the United States in training Latin American police and military in riot, subversion, and counterinsurgency techniques.[5] But from whatever source Latin American military and police learned their tactics, they were good at what they did.

The arsenal of weapons against "subversion" has grown steadily; Amnesty International reported in 1980 that the Colombian security forces were now employing fifty different torture techniques. Systematic, technically sophisticated torture is but one of the accusations the church has made against military governments. Repression of various sorts—including censorship and the shutdown of publications and radio stations, harassment, illegal break-ins, exile, imprisonment without the right of *habeas corpus*, and the disappearance of citizens—has also been objected to.

Basically, the rules of the political game have changed on a systematic basis. With it, the environment accompanying the game has changed too. Subtleties observed before the changes were no longer in effect. The right of sanctuary (if persons could make it to a church or a religious building, they were safe) was no longer observed in many places. Those offering sanctuary, sometimes begrudgingly, were subject to arrest, imprisonment, and the threat of death (as in the case of Father Gerald Whelan, a Holy Cross priest who was sentenced to death, a sentence that was forestalled by the efforts of President Theodore Hesburg of Notre Dame University and others).

Under the old rules, those who held power could be expected to exile political opponents who threatened conflict. The number of those exiled was often determined by the number of seats on the next plane out of the country. In the case of imprisoning one's opponents, rulers would not want to go "too far," because they feared that some day they might be deposed and held answerable.

Amnesty, too, was granted on an almost calendarlike basis. It is still granted now, but much less frequently and on a much more restricted basis. Fear of retaliation, a strong cultural tendency, is not a strong deterrent for the military.

The Catholic and mainline historical Protestant churches have become important counterweights to the abuses of human rights. Pentecostal groups, sects such as Jehovah's Witnesses, Seventh Day Adventists, and Mormons, and syncretist religious elements such as *macumbá* seldom involve themselves in human rights efforts in the five countries in question. Efforts to combat human rights violations have been made at international, regional, and national levels. At the international level churches have acted as reliable and sustained sources of information for the outside world. They have elicited informal and formal pressure from the Vatican and from other international bodies. They have also furnished considerable financial and material help.

From an organizational perspective the Catholic and Protestant churches offer a number of advantages in that they are transnational bodies. They serve as reliable sources of information in an atmosphere where information about human rights violations is carefully guarded. The five regimes strongly resisted efforts by fact-finding groups. Amnesty International, the Organization of American States (OAS), the Bertrand Russell Peace Foundation, the United Nations Commission on Human Rights, and ad hoc groups from the Vatican, the U.S. State Department, and other organizations typically encounter resistance to or denial of requests for investigations.

The southern tier churches have sent information to other countries through formal and informal networks. The National Council of Churches (New York), the U.S. Catholic Conference (Washington), the World Council of Churches (Geneva), and the Pontifical Commission on Justice and Peace (Rome)—each with its own publications—have important channels for the information pouring from Latin America. So too have less formal organizations that have sprung up, such as the ecumenically-based Office on Latin America (Washington) and the North American Congress on Latin America (New York), and numerous other organizations such as the Sojourner Community (Washington).

They share concern about human rights along with other justice issues.

To stop this flow of information would be impossible but at times incoming and outgoing mail is subjected to "surveillance." At times in Bolivia a third of the normal incoming mail would be missing; sometimes the reason, though, was simply theft, not counterintelligence. Attempts to survey information from Latin America have taken place in the United States as well. Father Louis ("Mike") Colonnese, former director of the Latin American Bureau (LAB) of the U. S. Catholic Conference took it for granted that U. S. intelligence agents had bugged his office. In the middle of a conversation he would pick out a homing device from his desk, adjust the antenna, dial, and say, "See, this tells what channel they're on."[6]

With reliable information in hand, personnel from the Vatican, foreign embassies, and other international agencies can apply pressure on repressive governments. Usually these efforts to redress human rights violations are first attempted "diplomatically," when a visitor from Rome (Vatican), Geneva (WCC), or an ambassador visits a minister of foreign relations to discuss or protest the jailing or threatened expulsion of church personnel. (The majority of religious personnel in many Latin American countries are foreigners.)[7]

There are several reasons why such efforts have seldom had much success: 1) visitors frequently do not know all the facts of the situation and may have doubts about the ideology or orthodoxy of the aggrieved religious parties; 2) the foreign minister does not control the defense or interior ministries and may not like or approve of the behavior of the military and the police anyway; and 3) most visitors have little power over the host government, in the sense of posing a real threat.

In contrast to the informal efforts just described, formal international efforts of fact-finding, publication, and ultimately public pressures for reform of violations have had a somewhat stronger effect. Initiatives taken by church personnel have led to published reports by various international bodies of the specifics and extent of rights violations.

The threat of the loss of international esteem is no longer as strong a threat as it was once, as has been evidenced in the Philippines, Iran, Korea, El Salvador, Chile, and Guatemala. The response of Argentina to the 1980 OAS report was typical. The government categorically denied the validity of investigations leading to the contention that, among other things, that as many as fifteen thousand Argentinians had simply "disappeared." Nonetheless most observers believe that these international efforts have moderated or reduced the volume of human rights violations in Latin America. (It is noteworthy that in Argentina some of the grosser violations ceased after the OAS report.) International efforts have been most effective when reinforcing strong national initiatives.

At times individual cases have gained widespread international attention—for example, Bishop Pedro Casaldáliga, a Spaniard threatened with expulsion from Brazil, and Doctor Sheila Cassidy, an English Catholic doctor sentenced to long-term imprisonment in Chile but eventually released. Both have since published moving accounts of their interior lives and their personal commitments.[8] What sorts of persons pose a threat to military governments can be discerned in these accounts.

International church bodies most strongly aided human rights efforts in Latin America by contributing financial and material help. These groups sent millions of dollars in support of efforts for improving human rights in both the narrower and wider sense. European and North American churches have contributed large amounts of clothing and food as well.

In addition to formal and organizational initiatives, vigorous efforts have also been expended by informal groupings of persons who have come to know one another through shared interests. The tracing of these networks is intriguing. Network members met one another in the national and international commissions for Vatican II, or at similar congresses or conferences at summer institutes or seminars and courses in theology or the ministry. They continue to communicate with one another and disseminate new ideas.

Formation of one of the earliest networks grew out of the threat to Catholic intellectuals and activists that by 1970 had become widespread. The network was called MIAU, after the sound a cat makes when its tail is walked on. The group went out of existence, in part because its coordinator, Father Colonnese, was removed in 1971 as executive director of the Latin American Bureau. Other groups arose to fulfill the need for communication and publicity about human rights violations. The First Conference of Latin American Christians in Exile met in 1978 in Brussels. It is a grassroots organization set up to represent two million exiles. Another group, of key leadership figures, created HABEAS (Human Rights Group for Latin America and the Caribbean). Cardinal Arns of São Paulo and other leading Latin Americans started the group as a Mexican-based foundation.

Leadership at the regional level has been reinforced by the Latin American Episcopal Council (CELAM). The bishops stepped up their public condemnations of the abuses of power. At their meetings at Medellín and Puebla they discussed structures of injustice in Latin America. They pointed to the deeper underlying causes that engender the escalation of systematic violations of human rights: unjust economic structures, maldistribution of land and wealth, inadequate social and political participation by the poor in national life, and the pervasiveness of an ideology of national security that subjugates personal rights to elitist expediency.

Thus in the bishops' minds there is a connection between repression of rights and the desire of elites—especially wealthy elites—to maintain their power. There is also in their minds a connection between poverty and repression.

These statements were foreshadowed in pastoral letters from various bishops, especially in Chile, Brazil, and Argentina.[9] The bishops did not stop with simply calling for an end to repression and torture. More importantly, they urged secular leaders to make more radical changes: to effect a more equitable distribution of land and other resources, to respect worker organizations, to allow greater participation in the social order for the rural and urban poor, and to enforce laws impartially.

This vision led the way to the setting up of a whole new series of social and pastoral programs at the grassroots level and the establishment of church-sponsored organizations for the defense of human rights. The documents of the bishops and their commissions have received wide publicity. But until the awarding of the 1980 Nobel Peace Prize to Adolfo Pérez Esquivel, little attention was given to lay or grassroots leadership.

Human rights organizations have provided considerable assistance for the victims of violations of human rights and for the poor generally. But they have also caused serious tensions between church and state, and within the churches.

Military Doctrine

The second area of conflict between the church and the military is that of military doctrine. The church strongly opposes the ideology of national security, which identifies government, nation, and the military. It makes national security the highest goal of a country and it postulates a mentality of perpetual readiness for warfare.[10] It has led the military from being arbiter of the regime to being arbiter of the nation.

The church did not immediately comprehend or react to the shift in military doctrines, although an occasional chaplain in the 1960s underwent lengthy training at the Brazilian command school where the new doctrines formed the basis of much of the instruction. In 1968, the year of the Medellín conference, very few prophets saw what the military presence would mean. But Bishop Cándido Padín was one of those prophets.[11] His acquaintance with the Brazilian military led him to a study of the ideology (which he perceived to be new) prevailing in Brazilian military elites. Padín prepared a detailed analysis of new military doctrines given the unfamiliar title of the doctrine or ideology of national security.

He presented his analysis at the national meeting of the Brazilian bishops. The document he presented went unsigned by the Brazilian bishops. His argument was beyond the ken of most of them, a notable instance of cognitive dissonance (the inability to believe what is too far away from one's value system). Within a decade, bishops in Brazil and Latin America would understand what Padín was arguing. For many in the church, agreement with Padín would come not so much because of reasoning but because of painful experience, that of the repression of human rights, torture, and the disappearance of clerical, religious, and lay members. A new church was facing a new political environment.

By 1975, the first formal analysis of the doctrine of national security was made by an important subregional group within

CELAM, at the meeting of the Andean Regional Social Action Commission. But the topic was only a secondary one on the agenda. The three cardinals and nine bishops read and discussed the working paper on the doctrine of national security, as well as papers on other topics related to the military (extreme nationalism and the arms race).[12] In the intervening years before the Puebla Conference (1979), many other studies, statements, and discussions of military philosophy and conduct would be made within the Latin American church.

The official preparatory document leading up to the Puebla Conference reflected little of this debate because the document had been controlled tightly by conservative Archbishop (later Cardinal) López Trujillo. Nonetheless within the hectic two-week meeting at Puebla three of the twenty-two commissions interposed considerations of the military and their doctrine of national security. The problem was clearly on the minds of many bishops. In the end, they said:

> To those in the military we would reiterate what the Medellín conference told them: "They have a mission to guarantee rather than inhibit the political freedom of citizens." They should be mindful of their mission, which is to guarantee the peace and security of all. They should never abuse the force they possess. They should be the defenders of the force of right and law. They should also foster a societal life that is free, participatory, and pluralistic.[13]

The bishops at the Puebla Conference took up explicitly the question of national security in five places in the final document; the question was very much on their minds. They speak of the nature of the doctrine (§ 49); they define it (§ 547); they argue against it generally (§ 549) and specifically state that the ideology opposes a Christian view of human nature (§§ 12 and 1262).

The ideology of national security that the church opposed was changing its formulations, but the church was not fully aware of the changes. José Comblin and other intellectuals in the church saw the military ideology as primarily focusing on East-West conflicts. Military planners were shocked in 1973 by the Arab oil crisis and mounting external debts owed to banks outside their own sphere of influence. Military thinking turned to North-South conflicts rather than East-West. Argentina went to war with Britain. The church has not tracked well the shifts in military ideology.

Goals of Military Rule

Another area of conflict has to do with the goals of military rule. Two goals are singled out by the church: national development and what is called *armentismo*, "armamentism."[14] The church holds that development must be integral and universal—that is, applying to the whole person and to every person. Military rulers defined development differently among themselves. The two most prominent models were the Brazilian and the Peruvian. The Brazilian model tended to ignore the lower sectors of society. It was thought that they would benefit at a later date as a fallout effect of economic growth. The Peruvian model aimed at improving the conditions of the lower classes. The church, which by then proclaimed that preferential treatment should be given the poor, found itself more easily aligned with the Peruvian than the Brazilian model.[15]

Armentismo leads the military to continuously update and augment its military stock. Some attention was given by the church to the enhanced potential for warfare among nations caused by the arms race. But the church based its criticism of military buildup primarily on the argument that poorer countries can ill afford such expenditures. The needs of the masses are too great to be sacrificed for additional armaments.

Consequences of Military Rule

The last area of conflict has been over the consequences of military rule. This is a relatively new area of criticism for the church: only after a history of some years could a clear judgment be made on the effects of military rule. Moreover, in countries such as Brazil the economy was booming for a while and there was talk of an "economic miracle." Even so, the final assessment, whether made by church-related observers or by most social scientists, is the same: the masses (rural and urban poor) have borne the costs of development, and the privileged classes have advanced.[16] In most countries where the military has been in power, its rule has not really benefited the rural and urban working classes from the standpoint of improved real income levels or availability of public services. In fact, for many the situation is worse than it was in the mid-1960s.

There are some exceptions—select groups of skilled workers, for example. But the general picture is bleak. Even of Brazil, with its much publicized boom, Sylvia Ann Hewlett can say, "The existence of massive poverty, the extreme concentration of income, and the increase in inequality during recent years are now accepted facts of contemporary Brazilian development."[17]

The Military and Politics

In Latin America the military is an extensively political enterprise. Most countries there have been ruled at one time or other by the military. Many countries recognize, constitutionally or unofficially, the armed forces as moderators of the regime, meaning that the armed forces are the ultimate judges of what is constitutional or not, a power unknown in the United States.

In most Latin American nations the armed forces receive a sizeable portion of the national budget, more than most other governmental agencies, despite the fact that major wars are virtually unknown in this century. Attempts to cut military spending are almost always unsuccessful, at least in the long run. Military men on active duty or on leave often fill governmental positions. Aside from a few Caribbean or Central American countries, most Latin American nations pay officers well, both in salary and in benefits, relative to other professionals in their countries.

Salaries, arms purchases, moderator role, governmental positions—all these are the result of frequent and effective political action. Despite the myth of being apolitical, the military is one of the most highly political institutions in Latin America.

The church has been changing since the mid-1960s, but the Latin American military has been evolving for a considerably longer period. Changes took place in the professional character of the military in the late nineteenth or early twentieth century; additional and important changes occurred during World War II and the period immediately following it. These changes include:

major technological advances, new professionalism, new military doctrines, enhanced corporate character, and new identity and awareness of institutional interests.

A caution must be expressed lest the church or the military be thought to be monolithic. Among most progressive Catholics there is general agreement about positions taken at Medellín and Puebla (where the vote on the final document was unanimous), but there are diverse interpretations among Catholics and an even greater variety of behavior patterns. Among Latin American military officers there is an even greater variety of positions and behavior patterns. There is less agreement about doctrines and an ever greater number of factions among and between branches of the armed forces.

Given the problematic inherent in any attempt to study a semi-secret organization, at times it is difficult to ascertain the nature and extent of factions within a particular armed force. Glimpses are afforded by debates that take place in organizations such as the Clube Militar in Brazil or changes in political direction following a shuffling of chairs in a cabinet. These and other indications are sufficiently frequent to divulge the number of factions and the depth of cleavage among the factions. Often it is the little publicized, unsuccessful, and frequent coup attempts that are the best indicators of factionalism. (In Argentina alone there were sixteen unsuccessful coup attempts in one ten-year period).

Military rule in Latin America (except perhaps in Paraguay) is not rule by a *caudillo* with whom one bargains one's fate. Military regime means rule by a more or less faceless organization that has numerous power bases within it. Many of these power bases are hidden from public view. How are nonmilitary political activists to bargain with or attempt coalitions with such opaque political partners? In addition, the bureaucrats in power are armed and they are trained to use force. Unfortunately for many Nicaraguans under Somoza or Bolivians under García Meza, to name but two countries, armed bureaucrats used tactics (indiscriminate firepower) and weapons (tanks and fighter planes) designed for use against other armies, not against civilians.

Military rule in Latin America means a regime of military and civilian elites in government. Military men dominate in that mix when controlling the presidential office and when setting overall policy orientations. But civilians fill many more positions in government. Often these positions are key: thus the minister of planning in Brazil is sometimes thought of as more important than the president. Even in the heyday of the military takeover in Peru, military men in direct governmental positions numbered no more than 175. In countries such as Colombia, Venezuela, or the Dominican Republic, where the regime is said to be civilian, there are many military men (active, on leave, or retired) in government positions. Officers sometimes fill posts in the military and "coordinate" their policies and tactics with civilian counterparts. Thus military "civic action" planners influence and are influenced by civilian colleagues in regional and national offices of the ministry (or secretariat) of planning.

In many ways, then, the distinction between military and civilian regimes is blurred in Latin America. In a general way one may say that almost all regimes, including Cuba, in Latin America are military-civilian regimes. This does not negate what has been said about "military" government in Latin America but rather emphasizes that the military organization and its characteristics have to be taken into account when discussing governments in Latin America, no matter whether a civilian is president or not.

New military regimes seek legitimacy from civilian elites in the government. Under the old political rules, new regimes sought legitimacy from other key political groups in the political system, groups that represented the people. Civilian elites in government generally continue their support of military regimes, in part because the armed forces bring to the government goals and ways of acting that civilian governmental elites readily understand and agree with. The military knows how to manage the government because military officers understand bureaucratic procedures and generally act them out well. This makes civilian bureaucrats comfortable, unless, of course, they question goals and means.

The symbiosis of military-civilian elites in government and the elimination or delimitation of the democratic political process leaves military regimes without a widespread political base. More importantly, Latin American military governments often do not have extensive, reciprocal interfacing with civilian political elites. This leaves military regimes open to the likelihood of being blind and deaf to other political groups and to the needs and will of the people as articulated through political groups. The degree of blindness and deafness varies from country to country.

Given the changed nature of the Latin American military, what does it mean for such an organization to occupy the presidential office or to act as a shadow government? The corporate nature of the armed forces, the doctrine of national security, and preoccupation with preservation of corporate interests all have consequences on the character of military rule (or tutelage): 1) the exercise of political power is carried on by the military high command in an institutional manner; 2) democratic processes for the most part are done away with for an indefinite period; 3) political parties, labor unions, and student political organizations are proscribed or closely watched; 4) a political economy is established that sooner or later welcomes foreign investment, does away with many of the measures designed to protect national industry, and redistributes national income in terms that are negative for many workers; 5) the government intervenes in universities and "restructures" them according to military thinking or limits severely the political activities of faculty members and students; 6) published thought that is critical of the government is proscribed, daily censorship of the mass media is often imposed, and newspapers are frequently "restructured" to fit better the "needs of the people;" 7) new technical forms of repression are used that tend to have at least a mild terrifying effect on the nation, and punitive operations, sometimes on a grand scale, are conducted against dissidents of the regime.

Why new rules for the political game? Loveman and Davies observe: "According to the military leadership, the old political institutions and practices gave rise to corruption, failed to solve national problems, and allowed advance of internal subversion."[18] Further, as Edward Feit puts it:

The world, as they [military and civilian bureaucrats] perceive it, is essentially plagued by poor organization, and it is organization that can provide the means by which problems can be overcome. Organization is the key. The solution of problems is merely a matter of finding the right key for the particular lock. Conflicting factions and structures of bu-

reaucracy tend to center in the "right" organizational form
and the "right" persons to control the organization.[19]

Participatory politics is seen by the military organization as
sloppy and ineffectual, not at all in keeping with the values that it
holds dear. Moreover, the old politics produced chaos and
brought the nation close to ruin, anarchy, communism, et cetera.
Given the situation, the military had to step in and rule or, in the
current case of Colombia, Venezuela, Ecuador, El Salvador, and
the Dominican Republic, the armed forces had to keep a close
surveillance over what was happening in the political life of the
country. Security demanded it. So did the preservation of the
armed forces. And it is hard for the military to separate these two
elements of national life.

The Church and Politics

How did the church respond to "permanent" military rule and
subsequent changes in national political life? At first, awkwardly
and disparately: a statement of protest appeared from a beset
bishop here or a troubled bishop there (Jesús de López Lama in
Bolivia, Cándido Padín in Brazil). Then came group statements
with long lists of signers, clerical and lay, Catholic and Protestant. There would be other statements by national conferences of
bishops. Then in 1968 the bishops at the Medellín conference told
the military, in effect, to cool it, to go back to its old role: "The
military has a mission to guarantee rather than prohibit the political liberty of citizens."[20]

For the church, as for other political bodies in Latin America, it
was a matter of learning how to live with the new military. It took
time to size up the creature that had been growing in semisecrecy.
The church had not been paying attention to the characteristics of
a changed military. And despite its prophetic stance, it still does
not understand fully the new character of the military organization.

Whatever judgment one made of the political effectiveness of
the church before 1965, a new assessment is called for.[21] The rules
of the political game in many countries have changed and the
self-definition of the church has changed. How well does the con-

temporary church do in the political arena? Its performance varies from place to place. Many upper-level and grassroots leaders play a political role with expertise. However, many others flounder in political situations. They lose the political game and sometimes their resources, including their lives.

What the church lacks politically is a clear and explicit view of power/conflict and a realistic conception of the state as crafted by ruling elites. There are several reasons for this lack.

For one, elements within the church persist in thinking that the church should remain out of politics. Vatican officials have argued that to get into politics is to divide the church.

That view, regarded by many in Latin America as simplistic, was rejected at Puebla. Instead, the Latin American bishops stated clearly and forcefully: "The fact is that the need for the church's presence in the political arena flows from the very core of the Christian faith."[22]

Secondly, the ideological basing of the Latin American church, the theology of liberation, offers another reason for the lack of clarity about power and about the current practice of statehood in Latin America. Paradoxically, liberation ideology (which many claim is too political) is not at all clear about political realities. This is because liberation theology is largely undergirded by sociological analysis, with some economic analysis. Very few influential liberation authors discuss at length political power, policy-making, or the de facto practice of statecraft, the main concerns of political scientists.

What political thinking has gone into the liberation ideology has explicit ties with European "political theology," the type enunciated by Johannes Metz and others, German and Dutch intellectuals for the most part. That type of political theology tends to moralize about what should be; it seldom bothers itself with descriptions of how national political agents wield power or how national policy is formed. That moralizing tendency influences how the church conceives of the state. The organizational church thinks of the state and deals with it on the basis of a medieval conception of the state as "the administrator of the common good," as looking out for the common welfare of its citizens.[23] In reality, and this is crucial, the modern state in Latin America has been a corporate bureaucratic entity. In practice, the state looked out for its own corporate interests, not primarily the interests of its citizens.

This lack of attention to structural matters of power and conflict and to a realistic conception of the state severely limits the political effectiveness of the church. The church loses in the political arena when it assumes naively that the government is looking after the good of its citizens. Thus the Dominican government co-opted and corrupted Catholic cooperative movements and diffused church land reform efforts.

Corruption within the ranks (the Bolivian military government was described as a "kleptocracy"),[24] military defeat (the defeat of Argentina by Britain), and, above all, mounting external and internal pressures because national economies turned sour has forced some armed forces to abandon the presidential palace or at least to promise elections.

The resulting decompression and opening of the political arena has brought an easing of tensions between the church and the military in some countries. The church welcomes the greatly diminished occurrence of deaths and disappearances, even the recognition by the Argentinian military that such things have occurred. But church publications continue to report human rights violations in some areas of national life, notably labor organization, land reform, and among Amerindian populations.[25]

Both the military and the church promise to be prominent forces in Latin America throughout the 1980s. Both are going through a process of change and are adopting new ideologies. Whether they will enter into new disputes remains to be seen. At any rate, the outlines of potential conflict are marked off far more clearly than they were in 1964.

Conclusion

A New Era:
Leadership of the
Latin American Church

The Latin American church is leading the worldwide church into a new era. In the first few centuries of its existence the Christian church was a Mediterranean institution, one dominated by Mediterranean cultural preferences and thought patterns. Then, imperceptibly, the church became European, its ideology sealed by the fusion of Mediterranean philosophy with European theology.

Theology and the church today are entering a new age, one in which theologians are searching for a new synthesis. It is an era similar to the eleventh and twelfth centuries when philosophers and theologians began developing new methods and new systems. Out of their efforts Scholasticism was built, best represented by Thomas Aquinas's *Summa Theologiae* in the thirteenth century. In the searching that is taking place today, many partial theories and methods are proposed. Every eighteen months or so a Robinson, Bonhoeffer, Cox, Altizer, or Moltmann flash across the theological sky. By contrast, theology of liberation has not passed away as a fad; it is a current of thought that will contribute to a larger postmodern theological synthesis.

The reaffirmation of neo-Scholasticism imposed by Cardinal Merry del Val, Vatican secretary of state, in the nineteenth century and fostered by Roman theologians in this century took place just as many European Catholics and Protestants were seeking new forms of thought and expression in the philosophies of experience and other contemporaneous philosophies. They were searching for a new synthesis that would better explain the church in the modern world. They concerned themselves with the place of the believer in the world of science and technology. They also reflected on what role the church should play in the world. Their efforts were mightily advanced by John XXIII's convocation of Vatican II and his appeal for aggiornamento, renewal of the church.

European bishops dominated the agenda and the discussions of Vatican II. European intellectuals provided the theology that permeated conciliar documents. But Vatican II, the greatest event in the last four centuries of Catholicism, is the last "European" council. For the church is becoming global: its interests are worldwide and include cultural ways and political questions other than West European. The questions that the church raises are now questions arising from the Second and Third Worlds. And the Latin American church is leading the way in raising these issues.[1]

But Latin America has produced answers, as well. The burst of creative activity that marked Latin America in the 1960s and '70s produced notable intellectual creations, some of which have been accepted in other parts of the world and reshaped to mesh with local circumstances. Not all those creations were life-fostering; one, the doctrine of national security, has resulted in injury and death for thousands. Two of the creations—national security and the theology of liberation—are in direct conflict in attempting to explain and influence what should be taking place in social and political life.

The major Latin American creations were a surprise to observers in the U.S.A. and Europe, who had long been accustomed to seeing only derivative forms of thought in Latin America. Thus, at first, outside observers were slow to react to and even take seriously the theology of liberation, base Christian communities, the ideology of national security, and dependency analysis.

But the rate of interaction among intellectual creators, religious or secular, and their followers or critics is now so great that what would otherwise have taken decades to communicate and assimilate now takes only years. In the case of the church, beneath the surface activity of publishing, of teaching future leaders, and of disseminating new teachings and techniques to the masses lie networks of key diagnosticians, original thinkers, integrators, and reformers. They crisscross the skies of Latin America and beyond, bearing with them new ideas and promoting new solutions. A chief Latin American proponent of base Christian communities, José Marins, teaches clerical and lay ministers in the Philippines or the United States with almost as much frequency as he does in his native Brazil.

Center Stage in the Drama of Religion and Politics: Nicaragua

The difficulties faced by the churches of the Second and Third worlds are especially political in nature: how to relate themselves to the political environment. The inventive forces of the Latin American church have been applied in large measure to the questions of how to operate in environments that are uncertain or hostile.

The difficulties are many and the risks are great, with consequences reaching beyond national boundaries. Church leaders in Rome and in Washington are watching closely, as are groups as diverse as the CIA, the Latin American Institute in Moscow, and the *Wall Street Journal*.

The conflicts and hopes, the confusion and promise, of the contemporary Latin American church are nowhere more evident than in a tiny country that until recently contributed little creativity to the life of the church. Its lack of promise was understandable. One family with a giant guardian standing behind it dominated Nicaragua: the Somoza dynasty and the active support of the U.S. government.[2]

Some citizens, including many from the church, grew in their determination to gain freedom. The action of church leaders and the entry of many Christians into the ranks of the Sandinista liberation movement was decisive in bringing final victory over Somoza.[3] Of the three branches that came together to form the final Sandinista coalition, the one composed of committed Christians was the largest. They were to moderate gradually, at least at the beginning of the coalition, the extreme leftist positions of the early guerrillas.[4]

The insurrection was not the problem in Nicaragua. The choice was clear: all peaceful means had been used in attempting to gain freedom. The bishops of Nicaragua agreed and said so in public in early June 1979, two days before the final general strike. Nor was there a problem of choice following the Sandinista victory. All the bishops of Nicaragua urged Christians to actively support the Sandinista government in the reconstruction of the country. Nicaragua was not only torn by war in which forty thousand had died, eighty thousand had been wounded, and multitudes left homeless (in a population of 2.5 million). The country also lay partially devastated by an earthquake. Moreover many talented Nicaraguans had fled the country over the years. All able-bodied persons, especially trained ones, were needed. Christians, lay and clerical, entered government service in large numbers.

In Nicaragua the crisis in the church was identity: how closely could it be identified with the regime? It was an old dilemma for the church, but for new reasons. The church has always been in politics in Latin America, politics being the sea in which the church has to swim. But, for the most part, it was politics of survival, of organization-maintenance. The church had no ideology to undergird further involvement. Instead the Latin American church had chosen to emphasize the otherworldly aspects of its tradition. But now the Latin American church had a new ideology that validated and promoted "building up the world." It now had movement at the grass roots, new community structures, new ways for lay persons to shoulder leadership. The church was being pushed (and drawn) into a mysterious land where the outlines of a different society were not clearly seen. Would it be capitalist, socialist, or what?

The bishops, with the encouragement of Rome and certain elements within CELAM, chose to drop back at the border of the mystery;[5] then increasingly they offered critical comments on the performance and orientation of the Sandinista government. Many sisters and priests (especially from religious orders) and many committed lay persons elected to plunge in. They would help to make the outlines of a new society clearer, they believed.

("Making the future happen" described well their feelings.) The degree of involvement with the Sandinista enterprise varied from person to person (with some sitting in ministerial chairs and others attending local FSLN [Sandinista National Liberation Front] meetings) but they hardly differed in their degree of commitment and enthusiasm for the cause. They provide the only case in Latin America of large groups of Christians actively supporting an insurrection on its way to becoming a successful revolution.

In the process the Sandinistas and their followers were creating new myths and a utopian movement to follow the myths. The Sandinistas described part of the myth in a communiqué on religion.[6] They proposed that the Christian faith, by its very nature, leads its adherents to participation in the transformation of society.

That utopian view often clashed with public performance of the Sandinista government, in the minds of a number of observers, including John Paul II. By many accounts, the Sandinistas botched the papal visit to Nicaragua in early 1983 and television watchers saw John Paul II impatiently responding to government leaders and brushing aside Father Ernesto Cardenal, minister of culture.[7]

But which way is the transformation going? Key to an interpretation is the Sandinista determination to have one political party and one labor union. For some that could only mean one of two things: the Cuban model or the Mexican model. For many it would be an ominous choice: Cuba and communism, Mexico and authoritarianism. For North American progressives or Latin American leftists either choice would be inadequate or an unacceptable disappointment. But many in Nicaragua argue that for a long phase the revolution has to consolidate itself. Moreover it needs a period of time to raise participatory consciousness at the grassroots level.

Many in and outside Nicaragua are uncomfortable with the Sandinista myth, that of creating a new society, and will work to bring down the enterprise.[8] In one scenario, observers say that in the very process of withholding support, the U.S.A. and cautious backtrackers within the country will push the Sandinista leaders toward the attractive model of Cuban socialism. But Nicaragua by itself is too poor, too lacking in resources, to have a Cuban-style revolution. And one senses no willingness on the part of the Russians to pick up, directly or indirectly, the expense of another Cuba. Nicaragua will have to struggle to find its own way, as did Mexico more than sixty years earlier.

Models of Survival

Many other Latin American countries did not have the freedom to decide what forms of government they would prefer. Military leaders have imposed bureaucratic, authoritarian regimes. What form of political interaction will the church take in such an environment?

Because the church cannot match the military in terms of controlled violence, real or implied, how can it thrive in the shadow of a hostile state? Are there models for a church "in captivity"? Church leaders want a situation wherein the institution will not simply survive, treading water until rescue comes, but one wherein its members can flourish.

At the time of the Puebla conference discussion of models of coexistence turned to the Cuban model. Raúl Gómez Treto, president of the Cuban Association of the Laity, enthusiastically presented the Cuban model for the consideration of theologians and journalists present at the meeting during a CENCOS briefing session. He recounted the stages of evolution of church relationships with the Castro government from cooperation, confrontation, passive hostility, and then active cooperation. Likewise, Francisco Oves Fernández, archbishop of Havana, advocated at the same conference active cooperation in the revolutionary process.

Gómez Treto's presentation went largely unreported, an untypical reaction of press members present at the daily CENCOS meetings. Church leaders, for their part, react against the Cuban model not because of the stridency of Gómez Treto or other Cuban advocates. They are repelled by the relative lack of "success" of the Cuban church. Never a very religious people in terms of participation, Cuban Catholics have been decimated by a precipitous decline in clergy (from 723 in 1960 to 213 in 1980), lack of church influence upon younger Cubans, and active discrimination against practicing Christians.

By contrast, the Brazilian church follows in prominent details the model set by the Polish church: reach out to the masses, enliven their religious motivations, and encourage them to take an active part in society. Polish Catholics attempted to act by force of mass movement against the goals and the drift of the Polish Communist Party and government. Theirs was not the old-style revolution of waging guerrilla warfare, arming the masses, and storming the barricades. Nor did they seek direct debate with the government. Rather they acted as if they should have a labor union—and then they went ahead and formed one, as it were, spontaneously, before the eyes of civil authorities. They acted as if they had a right to strike, and they went out on strikes that have been forbidden.

It is no accident that a number of Brazilian labor leaders developed their ideologies and leadership skills in *comunidades de base*. Nor is it an accident that wives of workers, also members of *comunidades de base*, conducted the sort of public demonstrations proscribed by the Brazilian government. Apart from speculation about resemblances between Brazilian labor unions and the Solidarity movement, one notes that motivation for public political activity derives from the experience of living as church among the masses, both in Brazil and Poland.[9]

It is not as if the Brazilian church consciously planned the strengthening of labor unions or how the unions should make demands on the political system. Rather, in reaching out to the urban and rural poor, and empowering them for activity in church and in the world, the church enlivened them for activity in an unfriendly or hostile environment. The church in Brazil has come alive in ways far exceeding the church in Cuba.

One wonders if John Paul II saw parallels between the Brazilian and Polish churches. At all events his visit to Brazil gave him twelve days to absorb at first hand what was taking place there. In clear language and through symbolic gestures (embrace of Archbishops Lorsheider and Camara, among others), John Paul ratified the direction the Brazilian church is taking. He restored hope to many who felt beseiged in a hostile environment. He saw that the reaching out of the church to the people is regenerating the institution. Its efforts also are beginning to have an impact on society at large.

The struggles of the church in Latin America have pulled the church in the United States into Latin American conflicts. The U.S. Catholic Conference regularly takes stands on behalf of the embattled Latin American church, lobbying in Congress, the White House, and the State Department, testifying in Congress, and serving as a focal point in the networks of Christian activists attempting to influence the course of foreign policy.[10] The Catholic bishops spoke for the historical interests of Panama in the Canal debate and regularly take up positions on human rights violations. Modification of aid to the Salvadoran government resulted in part from the mobilization of political resources in the United States by many Christian groups, including the U.S. Catholic Conference, the National Council of Churches, and the Washington Office on Latin America. Thus, changes in the Latin American church have radiated beyond national boundaries, affecting political systems of other countries.

With the wounding of John Paul II and the assassination of Anwar Sadat by religious fanatics, the creation and growth of the Moral Majority, the religion and politics debate in the U.S. presidential campaign of 1984, the takeover of the Iranian regime by religious extremists, and the conflicts of the church and the military in Latin America, the question of religion and politics in our day has come center stage. And one of the dramas unfolding there for a long time to come will be that of the church in Latin America.

Notes

Chapter 1

1. For detailed efforts to examine the church in specific national contexts see Thomas C. Bruneau, *The Church in Brazil: The Politics of Religion* (Austin: University of Texas Press, 1982); Daniel H. Levine, *Religion and Politics in Latin America: The Catholic Church in Venezuela and Colombia* (Princeton University Press, 1981); Brian H. Smith, *The Church and Politics in Chile: Challenges to Modern Catholicism* (Princeton University Press, 1982). For recent general treatments of the Catholic Church in Latin America, see Penny Lernoux, *Cry of the People* (New York: Doubleday, 1980); Otto Maduro, *Religion and Social Conflicts* (Maryknoll, N.Y.: Orbis, 1982); Daniel H. Levine, ed., *Churches and Politics in Latin America* (Beverly Hills, Cal.: Sage, 1980). For earlier works on religion and society in Latin America, see Ivan Vallier, *Catholicism, Social Control, and Modernization* (Englewood Cliffs, N.J.: Prentice-Hall, 1970); Frederick C. Turner, *Catholicism and Political Development in Latin America* (University of North Carolina Press, 1971); Edward L. Cleary, ed., *Shaping a New World: An Orientation to Latin America* (Maryknoll, N.Y.: Orbis, 1971); Henry A. Landsberger, ed., *The Church and Social Change in Latin America* (University of Notre Dame Press, 1970); Emmanuel DeKadt, *Catholic Radicals in Brazil* (New York: Oxford, 1970); Thomas C. Bruneau, *The Political Transformation of the Brazilian Catholic Church* (New York: Cambridge, 1974); Thomas Sanders, "The Church in Latin America," *Foreign Affairs*, 48, 2 (1970). Several excellent review essays have appeared in *Latin American Research Review*: Gerhard Drejonka, "Religion and Social Change in Latin America," 6, 1 (1971) 53–72; Thomas C. Bruneau, "Power and Influence: Analyses of the Church in Latin America and the Case of Brazil," 8, 2 (1973) 25–51; Brian Smith, "Religion and Social Change," 10, 2 (1975) 3–34; Ralph della Cava, "Catholicism and Society in Twentieth-Century Brazil," 11, 2 (1976) 7–50; Daniel H. Levine, "Religion, Society, and Politics: The State of the Art," 16, 3 (1981) 185–209. Hans-Jurgen Priën provides an extensive bibliography on the church and

Latin America in *Die Geschichte des Christentums in Lateinamerika* (Göttingen: Vandenhoeck & Ruprecht, 1978), pp. 1188-1243. Two annotated bibliographies emphasize Protestantism in Latin America and include references to Roman Catholicism and to Latin America: John H. Sinclair, ed., *Protestantism in Latin America: A Bibliographic Guide* (S. Pasadena, Cal.: William Carey Library, 1976); Justo L. Gonzalez, *The Development of Christianity in the Latin Caribbean* (Grand Rapids: Eerdmans, 1969), pp. 125-29). For a review of current sources of information on the church in Latin America, see Penny Lernoux, "The Latin American Church," *Latin American Research Review*, 15, 2 (1980) 201-11.

2. W. Dayton Roberts, *Strachem of Costa Rica* (Grand Rapids: Eerdmans, 1971), p. 129.

3. Quoted in Roberts, *Strachem*, p. 130.

4. Ibid.

5. Enrique Dussel treats Catholic Action in *Hipótesis para una historia de la Iglesia en América Latina* (Barcelona: Estrela-IEPAL, 1967), pp. 144-46. Arthur Alonso has written a general treatment: *Catholic Action and the Laity* (St. Louis: Herder, 1961). Helpful, although dated, coverage is provided by Gordon F. Anderson, "The Development of Catholic Action, with Special Reference to Latin America" (New York: Union Theological Seminary, S.T.M. thesis, 1960). See also Carlos Alberto de Medina, *Participação e Igreja: Estudo dos movimentos e associações de leigos* (Cuernavaca: Centro Intercultural de Documentación, 1972); Oscar Domínguez Correa, *El campesino chileno y la Acción Católica Rural* (Fribourg: Oficina Internacional de Investigaciones de FERES, 1961); Elwood R. Gotshall, "Catholicism and Catholic Action in Mexico, 1929-1941: A Church's Response to a Revolutionary Society and the Politics of the Modern World" (University of Pittsburgh, Master's thesis, 1970).

6. For a description of the relationship of the church to labor, see Alexis U. Florini and Annette F. Strefbold, *The Uncertain Alliance: The Catholic Church and Labor in Latin America* (Miami: University of Miami Press, 1973).

7. *Tercera Semana Interamericana de Acción Católica* (Lima and Chimbote, 1953). See also William J. Coleman, *Latin American Catholicism: A Self-Evaluation* (Maryknoll, N.Y.: Maryknoll Publications, 1958), and Helmut Gnadt Vitalis, *The Significance of Changes in Latin American Catholicism since Chimbote* (Cuernavaca: Centro Intercultural de Documentación, 1969).

8. Vitalis, *Significance of Changes*, no. 2, pp. 1-19.

9. *A Theology of Liberation* (Maryknoll, N.Y.: Orbis, 1973), pp. 45-77.

10. A vivid insight into many aspects of this missionary influx is provided by Gerald Costello, *Mission to Latin America: The Successes and Failures of a Twentieth-Century Crusade* (Maryknoll, N.Y.: Orbis, 1979).

11. John Considine, *A Call for Forty Thousand* (New York: Longmans Green, 1946).

12. Interview, April 2, 1971.

13. Ivan Vallier, "The Roman Catholic Church: A Transnational Actor," in Robert O. Keohane and Joseph S. Nye, eds., *Transnational Relations and World Politics* (Harvard University Press, 1972), p. 131.

14. Ivan Vallier and a graduate student assistant conducted a religious leadership network study in Latin America at the end of the 1960s. Both died before his findings and analysis of results could be completed.

15. See Sergio Torres and Virginia Fabella, eds., *The Emergent Gospel: Theology from the Underside of History* (Maryknoll, N.Y.: Orbis, 1978); Kofi Appiah-Kubi and Sergio Torres, eds., *African Theology en Route* (Orbis, 1979); Virginia Fabella, ed., *Asia's Struggle for Full Humanity* (Orbis, 1980); Sergio Torres and John Eagleson, eds., *The Challenge of Basic Christian Communities* (Orbis, 1981); Virginia Fabella and Sergio Torres, eds., *Irruption of the Third World* (Orbis, 1983).

Chapter 2

1. Norman Gall, *Pueblo de Dios* (Caracas: Monte Avila, 1970).

2. See, for example, Roberto Oliveros Maqueo, *Liberación y teología: Génesis y crecimiento de una reflexión (1966-76)* (Mexico City: Centro de Reflexión Teológica, 1977), pp. 119ff.

3. For a discussion of the notion of marginality, see Alejandro Portes, "Latin America: Social Structures and Sociology," *Annual Review of Sociology,* 7 (1981) 236-41, and Lisa Peattrie and José A. Aldrete-Haas, "Marginal Settlements in Developing Countries," ibid., pp. 157-75.

4. "Presencia de la Iglesia en el proceso de cambio en América Latina," *Signos de renovación* (Lima: CEP, 1969), p. 38.

5. Maryknoll, N.Y., Orbis, 1975.

6. Religious News Service, quoted in Gerald Costello, *Mission to Latin America* (Maryknoll, N.Y.: Orbis, 1979), p. 146.

7. Hernán Prada prepared a useful chronicle of the Medellín conference, one that imparts a sense of the meeting: *Crónica de Medellín: Segunda Conferencia General del Episcopado Latino-americano* (Bogotá: Indo-American Press Service, 1975).

8. *Crónica,* pp. 185-86.

9. Second General Conference of Latin American Bishops, *The*

Church in the Present-Day Transformation of Latin America in the Light of the Council, vol. 1: *Position Papers* (Washington: U.S. Catholic Conference, 1970). (Volume 2: *Conclusions*.)

10. References for dependency analysis are found in chap. 3, note 25, below. Questions about internal colonialism are treated in J. Walton, "Internal Colonialism: Problems of Definition and Measurement," *Latin American Urban Research*, 5 (1975) 29-50. See also Alan Gilbert, "The State and Regional Income Disparities in Latin America," in David J. Robinson, ed., *Studying Latin America: Essays in Honor of Preston E. James* (Ann Arbor: UMI Monographs, 1980), pp. 215-44.

11. *Conclusions*, Document 4, §9, and Document 14, §2.

12. *Boletín CELAM*, nos. 15 and 16 (1968).

13. *Une église en état de péché mortel* (Paris: Grasset, 1968), p. 106.

14. Enrique Dussel composed a lengthy chronicle and analysis of the decade from 1968 to 1978: *De Medellín a Puebla: Una década de sangre y esperanza* (Mexico City: Centro de Estudios Ecuménicos, 1979) in English see Dussel's *A History of the Church in Latin America: Colonialism to Liberation* (Grand Rapids: Wm. B. Eerdmans, 1981). See also José Marins et al., eds., *Práxis de los Padres de América Latina: Documentos de las Conferencias Episcopales de Medellín a Puebla* (Bogotá: Paulinas, 1978).

15. Prada, *Crónica*, p. 233.

16. Collections of documents of social activist priests are contained in *Social Activist Priests: Chile* and *Social Activist Priests: Colombia, Argentina*, LADOC Keyhole Series, nos. 5 and 6, respectively (Washington: U.S. Catholic Conference, n.d.). The bi-monthly publication *LADOC* (Lima, Peru) regularly publishes in English statements of bishops and activist groups of Latin America. For ONIS, see Jeffrey Klaiber, *Religion and Revolution in Peru* (University of Notre Dame Press, 1977), and M. G. Macauley, "Ideological Change and Internal Cleavages in the Peruvian Church: Change, Status Quo, and the Priest: The Case of ONIS" (Notre Dame University, Ph.D. dissertation, 1972). See also Michael Dodson, "The Christian Left in Latin American Politics," in Daniel H. Levine, ed., *Churches and Politics in Latin America* (Beverly Hills, Cal.: Sage, 1980), pp. 111-34; Ivan Vallier, "Radical Priests and Revolution," in Douglas Chalmers, ed., *Changing Latin America: New Interpretations of its Politics and Society* (Montpelier, Vermont: Capital City Press, 1972), and Mary Mooney, "The Role of the Church in Peruvian Political Development" (University of Windsor, M.A. thesis, 1976).

17. See, for example, Peruvian Bishops Commission for Social Action, *Between Honesty and Hope* (Maryknoll, N.Y.: Orbis, 1969); *The*

Church at the Crossroads: Christians in Latin America, From Medellín to Puebla, 1968-78 (New York: IDOC International, 1978); *Signos de lucha y esperanza: Testimonios de la Iglesia en América Latina, 1973-78* (Lima: CEP, 1978); Marins, *Praxis;* and back issues of *LADOC.*

18. Puebla, *Final Document,* §§ 64-70. The text cited here is the English translation authorized by the U.S. National Conference of Catholic Bishops' Committee for the Church in Latin America, contained in John Eagleson and Philip Scharper, eds., *Puebla and Beyond* (Maryknoll, N.Y.: Orbis, 1979).

Chapter 3

1. Puebla, *Final Document,* §§ 26, 41, 189, 261, 321, 329, 351-55, 452, 475, 479-506, 696, 895, 979, 1026; John Paul II, Opening Address of the Puebla Conference, section 3; General Audience in Rome, Feb. 14, 1979, and esp. General Audience in Rome, Feb. 21, 1979 (published in the English edition of *Osservatore Romano* for Feb. 19 and 26, 1979, respectively); *Redemptor Hominis,* passim. See also José A. Linares, "Liberación según Juan Pablo Segundo," *Ciencia Tomista,* vol. 106, no. 347, pp. 161-91.

2. Reactions, positive and negative, to liberation theology are numerous. They range from Kenneth Hamilton's judgment in "Liberation Theology: Lessons Positive and Negative," in Carl E. Armering, ed., *Evangelicals and Liberation* (Grand Rapids: Baker, 1977), p. 124: "That liberation theology is a heresy I believe to be beyond question," to more favorable reactions in the same volume. Robert McAfee Brown has catalogued critiques of liberation theology in his *Theology in a New Key: Responding to Liberation Theology* (Philadelphia: Westminster, 1978), pp. 102-31. Dennis P. McCann has written a full-length critique of the theology of liberation from the perspective of social ethics: *Christian Realism and Liberation Theology: Practical Theologies in Creative Conflict* (Maryknoll, N.Y.: Orbis, 1981).

3. A comprehensive bibliographic guide to Latin American theology has begun appearing yearly, *Bibliografía teológica comentada,* from the Instituto Superior Evangélico de Estudios Teológicos, Buenos Aires. A bibliographical resource from Spain is *Actualidad bibliográfica de filosofía y teología.* A valuable guide to works before 1975 is *Sociología de la religión y teología* (Madrid: Cuadernos para el Diálogo, 1975). For works in Portuguese, the Brazilian review *Atualização* publishes annually its *Bibliografía teológica brasileira.* Three other bibliographies of high quality but more limited scope are Therrin C. Dahlin, Gary Gillum, and Mark L. Glover, *The Catholic Left in Latin America: A Comprehen-*

sive Bibliography (Boston: Hall, 1981); Hans-Jurgan Priën, *Die Geschichte des Christentums in Lateinamerika* (Göttingen: Vanderhoeck & Ruprecht, 1970); and Lambros Comitas, *The Complete Caribbeana, 1900-1975* (Millwood, N.Y.: KTO Press, 1977). J. Andrew Kirk has compiled a useful select bibliography that emphasizes Protestant contributions to liberation theology in his *Liberation Theology: An Evangelical View from the Third World* (Atlanta: Knox, 1979), pp. 228-37. To his list should be added Kirk's own work and recent books by Protestants of varying traditions: Daniel L. Migliore, *Called to Freedom: Liberation Theology and the Future of Christian Doctrine* (Philadelphia: Westminster, 1980) and Theodore Runyon, ed., *Sanctification and Liberation: Liberation Theology in the Light of Wesleyan Tradition* (Nashville: Abingdon, 1981). See also John H. Sinclair, ed., *Protestantism in Latin America: A Bibliographical Guide* (S. Pasadena, Cal.: William E. Carey Library, 1976).

4. New York, Continuum, 1968.

5. Maryknoll, N.Y., Orbis, 1973.

6. See chap. 1, note 15, above, and Basil Moore, ed., *Black Theology: The South African Voice* (London: Hurst, 1973).

7. For a discussion of what constitutes ideology, see James M. Malloy and W. R. Campbell, "Ideology in an Action Framework: An Approach to Communist Political Behavior," *Occasional Papers in Political Science,* no. 3 (University of Rhode Island Press, 1968).

8. Roberto Oliveros Maqueo, *Liberación y teología: Génesis y crecimiento de una reflexión (1966-1976)* (Mexico City: Centro de Reflexión Teológica, 1977), pp. 344-72.

9. McAfee Brown has a helpful discussion of the antecedents of Protestant and Orthodox liberation thought in his *Theology in a New Key,* pp. 35-49. See also Edward Duff, *The Social Thought of the World Council of Churches* (New York: Association, 1956) and Paul Bock, *In Search of Responsible World Society: The Social Teaching of the World Council of Churches* (Philadelphia: Westminster, 1974).

10. Fremantle, Gremillion, and O'Brien and Shannon present overviews of Catholic social teaching with selection of documents. Guerry, Calvez and Perrin, Calvez, and Charles provide systematic presentation of Catholic social teaching. Aubert analyzes much of the evolution of the social teaching of the church and offers useful bibliographical references. Anne Fremantle, *The Social Teaching of the Church* (New York: Mentor-Omega, 1963); Joseph Gremillion, *The Gospel of Peace and Justice: Catholic Social Teaching since Pope John* (Maryknoll, N.Y.: Orbis 1976); David O'Brien and Thomas A. Shannon, *Renewing the Earth: Catholic Documents on Peace, Justice, and Liberation* (Garden City,

N.Y.: Doubleday Image, 1977); Emile Guerry, *The Social Doctrine of the Catholic Church* (New York: Alba, 1961); Jean-Ives Calvez and Jacques Perrin, *The Church and Social Justice: The Social Teaching of the Popes From Leo XIII to Pius XII* (London: Burns and Oates, 1961); Jean-Ives Calvez, *The Social Thought of John XXIII* (Chicago: Regnery, 1965); Rodger Charles, *The Christian Social Conscience* (Hales Corners, Wis.: Clergy Book Service, 1970); and Jean-Marie Aubert, *Pour une théologie de l'âge industriel* (Paris: Cerf, 1971). On the evolutionary character of Catholic school teaching John Coleman, S.J., "Development of Church Social Teaching," *Origins* 11, 3 (June 4, 1981) 34-41.

11. *Rerum Novarum,* § 20.

12. *Quadragesimo Anno,* § 50.

13. Ibid., § 109.

14. Ibid., § 120.

15. Ibid., § 132.

16. *Social Doctrine,* p. 286.

17. Letter, *Sertum Laetitiae,* Nov. 1, 1939.

18. *Gaudium et Spes,* § 69.

19. *Populorum Progressio,* part 1, § 26.

20. Medellín, "Peace," § 14.

21. For a discussion of the concept of praxis as used by Latin American social scientists, see Edward L. Cleary and Germán Garrido-Pinto, "Applied Social Science, Teaching, and Political Action," *Human Organization,* 36, 3 (Fall 1977) 270. For orthopraxis, see Robert L. Kinast, "Orthopraxis: Starting Point for Theology," *Proceedings of the Catholic Theological Society of America* (1983) 29-44.

22. *An Introduction to Philosophy* (New York: Sheed and Ward, 1930), pp. 82-83 and 98-99.

23. For a discussion of some key differences in social science in Latin America and the U.S.A., see Cleary and Garrido-Pinto, "Applied Social Science," pp. 269-71. For an excellent overview, see Alejandro Portes and William Canak, "Latin America: Social Structures and Sociology," in Ralph H. Turner and James F. Short, Jr., eds., *Annual Review of Sociology,* vol. 7 (Palo Alto, Cal., 1981), pp. 225-48.

24. For a helpful discussion of Marxian analysis in liberation theology, see Joseph Laishley, "Theological Trends: The Theology of Liberation I and II," *The Way,* 17, 3 (July 1977) 217-28 and 17, 4 (Oct. 1977) 301-11. See also the statement of a major proponent of liberation theology: Segundo Galilea, "The Theology of Liberation," *Lumen Vitae,* 33, 3 (1978) 342.

25. Since the original work of Caio Prado, Jr., Sergio Bagú, Florestán

Fernandes, André Gunder Frank, Raúl Prebisch, and Celso Furtado, a large body of literature on dependency has grown up. Peter Evans offers a useful bibliography in *Dependent Development: The Alliance of Multinational, State, and Local Capital in Brazil* (Princeton University Press, 1979), pp. 331-51. The debate continues especially in the pages of the *Latin American Research Review*. For research on multinational corporations, see Peter B. Evans, "Recent Research on Multinational Corporations," in Ralph H. Turner and James F. Short, Jr., eds., *Annual Review of Sociology,* vol. 7 (Palo Alto, Cal., 1981), pp. 199-223. Reviews of early literature on dependency are provided by Joseph Kahl, *Modernization, Exploitation, and Dependency* (New Brunswick, N.J.: Transaction, 1976); Fernando Henrique Cardoso, "The Consumption of Dependency Theory in the United States," *Latin American Research Review* 12, 3 (1977) 7-24; and Cardoso, "Current Theories of Latin American Development and Dependency: A Critique," *Boletín de Estudios Latino-americanos y del Caribe,* 22 (June 1977) 5-64. Among other critiques, see Philip O'Brien, in Ivar Oxaal et al., eds., *Beyond the Sociology of Development: Economy and Society in Latin America and Africa* (London: Routledge and Kegan Paul, 1975) and Harold Blakemore, "Limitations of Dependency: An Historian's View and Case Study," *Boletín de Estudios Latino-americanos y del Caribe,* 18 (June 1975) 74-87. For a discussion of the weaknesses of liberation theologians' use of dependency theory, see Michael Dodson, "Liberation Theology and Christian Radicalism in Contemporary Latin America," *Journal of Latin American Studies,* 11, 1 (1979) 203-33, esp. 208-14. Specific suggestions for the improvement of dependency analysis are offered by Steven Jackson et al., "An Assessment on Empirical Research on *Dependencia,"* *Latin American Research Review,* 14, 3 (1979) 7-28, esp. 22; and C. Richard Bath and Dilmus Jones, "Dependency Analysis of Latin America," *Latin American Research Review,* 11, 3 (1976) 3-54, esp. 33-36.—The *Latin American Research Review* has provided a forum for dependency theory, especially as *dependendistas* attempted to criticize one another's formulations and to recast dependency theory. For reviews of later formulations of dependency perspectives, see a series of articles forming a symposium on dependency, *Latin American Research Review,* 17, 1 (1982) 115-72.

26. See, for example, the Introduction in J. J. Villamil, ed., *Transnational Capitalism and National Development: New Perspectives on Development* (Hassocks, Sussex: Harvester, 1979); David G. Becker, *The New Bourgeoisie and the Limits of Dependency: Mining, Class, and Power in "Revolutionary" Peru* (Princeton University Press, 1983); and Sidney W. Mintz, "The So-Called World System: Local Initiative and Local Response," *Dialectical Anthropology,* 2, 4 (Nov. 1977) 253-70.

27. For an attempt to supply strategies to overcome dependency, see Heraldo Munoz, ed., *From Dependency to Development: Strategies to Overcome Development and Inequality* (Boulder: Westview, 1982).

28. John Browett, "Out of Dependency Perspectives," *Journal of Contemporary Asia,* 12, 2 (1982) 146.

29. See, for example, Leonardo Boff, *Liberating Grace* (Maryknoll, N.Y.: Orbis, 1979), pp. 67–72.

30. Faculty Seminar, Aquinas Institute of Theology, March 14, 1979.

31. *Liberación,* pp. 158–59.

32. *Theology in a New Key,* pp. 62–63.

33. *Our Idea of God* (Maryknoll, N.Y.: Orbis, 1974).

34. *Our Idea,* pp. 3–19.

35. In addition to Segundo, see Antonio Pérez-Esclarín, *Atheism and Liberation* (Maryknoll, N.Y.: Orbis, 1978).

36. *Gaudium et Spes,* § 19.

37. Thomas G. Sanders gives an excellent introduction to Freire's methods: "The Paulo Freire Method: Literacy Training and Concientización," *American Universities Field Service Reports,* West Coast South America Series, 15, 1 (1968).

38. Interviews at Florida International University, Miami, Nov. 10–31, 1979.

39. "Antecedentes para el estudio de la teología de la liberación (comentario bibliográfico)," *Tierra Nueva* (Bogotá) 1, 2; 1, 3; 2, 5 (1972–73).

40. Montevideo, MIEC-JECI, 1969.

41. Hugo Assmann in *Theology for a Nomad Church* (Maryknoll, N.Y.: Orbis, 1976), p. 8, says: "A theology of liberation began to take shape only after the Medellín conference in a series of occasional articles and more explicitly in proceedings of other conferences." In a footnote he refers to conferences held in 1970 and later years.

42. The mimeographed paper is in the archives of the Centro de Estudios Bartolomé de Las Casas, Lima.

43. *Lineas pastorales de la Iglesia en América Latina* (Lima: CEP, 2nd ed., 1976).

44. Included in *In Search of the Theology of Development* (Lausanne: SODEPAX, 1969).

45. *Theological Studies,* 31, 2 (1970) 243–61.

46. Interview, June 1978.

47. *Mensaje* (Chile), *Páginas* (Peru), *Diálogo Social* (Panama), *SIC* (Venezuela), *Diálogo* (Guatemala), *ECA* (El Salvador), and *Servir* (Mexico).

48. *Liberación y cautiverio* (Mexico City: Encuentro Latinoamericano de Teología, 1975).

49. Philadelphia: Fortress, 1975, p. 166.

50. "La teología," *Los católicos holandeses* (Bilbao: Desclée de Brouwer, 1970), p. 29.

51. See, for example, *Historia de la Iglesia en América Latina* (Barcelona: Nova Terra, 3rd ed., 1974); *Disintegración de la cristiandad colonial y liberación* (Salamanca: Sígueme, 1978); and *El episcopado latinoamericano y la liberación de los pobres, 1504-1620* (Mexico City: Centro de Reflexión Teológica, 1979).

52. See, for example, Enrique Dussel, *History and Theology of Liberation* (Maryknoll, N.Y.: Orbis, 1976).

53. Philip Scharper discusses the political aspects of theology in "Toward a Politicized Christianity," *Commonweal* (June 16, 1978), pp. 392-99.

54. *Doing Theology*, p. 93.

55. *Praxis of Liberation and Christian Faith* (San Antonio: Mexican-American Cultural Center, 1976), p. 19. See also *A Theology of Liberation*, pp. 45-50.

56. "Trends II," p. 304.

57. *Doing Theology*, p. 102.

58. *Theology in a New Key*, pp. 84-85.

59. Gutiérrez, *A Theology of Liberation*, pp. 294-96.

60. Ibid., p. 295.

61. "Theology of Liberation," p. 349.

62. Ibid., p. 349.

63. See chap. 4, "Salvation and Conscientization," in Letty Russell, *Human Liberation in a Feminist Perspective* (Philadelphia: Westminster, 1974), pp. 104-31.

64. "Theology of Liberation," p. 346.

65. Final Document, Introduction to *Conclusions*, §6.

66. "Theology of Liberation," p. 346.

67. Introduction to *Conclusions*, §6.

68. "Theology of Liberation," pp. 346-47.

69. Justo L. González and Catherine G. González, *Liberation Preaching: The Pulpit and the Oppressed* (Nashville: Abingdon, 1980), pp. 38-48.

70. *Theology in a New Key*, pp. 88-89. See also José Severino Croatto, *Liberación y libertad: Pautas hermenéuticas* (Buenos Aires: Mundo Nuevo, 1973).

71. See Míguez Bonino, *Doing Theology*, and Moltmann, "An Open Letter to José Míguez Bonino," *Christianity and Crisis* (March 29, 1975), pp. 57-63.

72. *A Theology of Human Hope* (New York: Corpus, 1969).

73. Quoted by Alfred Hennelly, "Apprentices in Freedom: Theology since Medellín," *America* (May 29, 1978): 418.

74. Sobrino, *Christology at the Crossroads: A Latin American Approach* (Maryknoll, N.Y.: Orbis, 1978); Boff, *Jesus Christ Liberator* (Orbis, 1978).

75. New York, Seabury, 1979.

76. New York, Seabury, 1980; see esp. part 4.

77. A Theology of Liberation, p. 203; *We Drink From Our Own Wells* (Maryknoll, N.Y.: Orbis, 1984).

78. Bogotá, CELAM Departamento de Pastoral.

79. Madrid, Editorial Cristiandad, 1979 (first published in 1974); see also his *Seguimiento de Cristo* (Bogotá: Paulinas, 1978) and *El rostro de Dios* (Petrópolis: Vozes, 1979).

80. For a discussion of early formulations of liberation ecclesiology, see T. Howland Sanks and Brian H. Smith, "Liberation Ecclesiology: Praxis," *Theological Studies*, 38, 1 (March 1977) 3-38.

81. Segundo, *The Community Called Church* (Maryknoll, N.Y.: Orbis, 1973); Boff, *Ecclesiogénesis: Las comunidades de base reinventan la Iglesia* (Santander: Sal Terrae, 2nd. ed., 1980).

82. See, for example, Brown, *Theology in a New Key*, pp. 80-85.

83. *The Coming of the Third Church* (Maryknoll, N.Y.: Orbis, 1977).

84. "Apprentices," p. 421.

85. Ibid.

86. Maryknoll, N.Y., Orbis, 1977 (both works).

87. See The Final Statement of the Ecumenical Dialogue of Third World Theologians. Dar es Salaam, Tanzania, August 5-12, 1976 in Sergio Torres and Virginia Fabella, M.M., eds., *The Emergent Gospel: Theology from the Underside of History* (Maryknoll, N.Y.: Orbis Books, 1978), pp. 259-71.

88. See Thomas E. Quigley, ed., *Freedom and Unfreedom in the Americas: Toward a Theology of Liberation* (New York: IDOC, 1971).

89. See Sergio Torres and John Eagleson, eds., *Theology in the Americas* (Maryknoll, N.Y.: Orbis, 1976).

90. See Cornel West, Caridad Guidote, and Margaret Coakley, eds. *Theology in the Americas: Detroit II Conference Papers* (Maryknoll, N.Y.: Orbis Probe, 1981).

91. Proceedings of the conference have been published in Sergio Torres and John Eagleson, eds., *The Challenge of Basic Christian Communities* (Maryknoll, N.Y.: Orbis, 1981).

92. Conference papers are published in Sergio Torres and Virginia Fabella, eds., *Doing Theology in a Divided World* (Maryknoll, N.Y.: Orbis, 1985).

93. See, for example, J. M. Aubert et al., *Théologies de la libération en Amérique Latine* (Paris: Beauchesne, 1974).

Chapter 4

1. Puebla, *Final Document,* §629.

2. A growing body of literature about *comunidades eclesiales de base* has developed. Among the more useful works are *Basic Christian Communities,* LADOC (Latin American Documentation) Keyhole Series, no. 14 (Washington: U.S. Catholic Conference, 1976); *Basic Communities in the Church* (Brussels: Pro Mundi Vita, 1976); Thomas C. Bruneau, "The Catholic Church and Development in Latin America," *World Development,* vol. 8, nos. 7 and 8 (July-Aug. 1980), pp. 535-44, and "Basic Christian Communities in Latin America: Their Nature and Significance (especially in Brazil)," in Daniel H. Levine, ed., *Churches and Politics in Latin America* (Beverly Hills, Cal.: Sage, 1981), pp. 225-37; Sergio Torres and John Eagleson, eds., *The Challenge.* See also a lengthy series of manuals and expositions of aspects of base Christian communities written by José Marins and a team of experts and published by Ediciones Paulinas, Bogotá; also, CELAM, *Comunidades cristianas de base* (Bogotá: Indo-American Press, 1970); Patricia Van Dorp and Heriberto Berger, *Comunidades cristianas de base: estudio teológico y sociológico* (Santiago: Centro Bellarmino, 1972); René Laurentin, *L'Amérique latine: A l'heure de l'enfantement* (Paris: Seuil, 1968), chaps. 4, 10, and 12.

3. Alfredo Kunz, "A BCC in a Rural Setting," LADOC, *Basic Christian Communities,* pp. 32-34.

4. José Marins, "Basic Christian Communities in Latin America," LADOC, *Basic Christian Communities,* pp. 1-12.

5. Dom Aldo Gerna, "How Our BCC Evolved," LADOC, *Basic Christian Communities,* pp. 13-16.

6. Francisco Bravo, *The Parish of San Miguelito in Panama* (Cuernavaca: Centro Intercultural de Documentación, 1966).

7. Interview, June 7, 1979.

8. Interview, June 6, 1979.

9. Ibid.

10. Interview, June 6, 1979; see also his "Basic Christian Communities," LADOC, *Basic Christian Communities,* p. 7.

11. Interview, Jan. 28, 1979.

12. Cornelia Butler Flora furnishes a bibliography on pentecostalism with special reference to Latin America in *Pentecostalism in Latin America* (Rutherford, N.J.: Farleigh Dickinson University Press, 1976), pp. 269-73. See also Flavio Siebeneichler, *Catolicismo popular—Pentecostismo—Kirche: Religion in Lateinamerika* (Frankfurt: Lang, 1976).

13. Interviews, Puebla, Jan. 28 to Feb. 13, 1979.

14. Interview, May 12, 1976.

15. Interview, Feb. 10, 1980.

16. Interview, Nov. 5, 1979.

17. Interview, March 20, 1980.

18. Plenary session, Puebla General Conference, Feb. 7, 1979.

19. Interview, June 28, 1979.

20. Symposium on New Strategy for Catholic Church Entry into Latin American Society, Latin American Studies Association Eighth National Meeting, Pittsburgh, April 6, 1979; Session on Conflict of Loyalty: Political Polarization in the Catholic Church in Latin America, Latin American Studies Association Ninth National Meeting, Bloomington, Ind., Oct. 19, 1980. See also Gerardo Viviers, "Christian Political Witness of the Church of the Poor: A Study of the Political Ecclesiology of CEBs in Brazil," Ph.D. dissertation, Princeton Theological Seminary, 1983.

21. *LADOC*, 10, 5 (May/June 1980) 12.

22. Puebla, *Final Document,* §1263.

23. Interview, Feb. 10, 1979.

24. Puebla, *Final Document,* §361.

25. Ibid., §263.

26. Informal press conference, Puebla, Feb. 2, 1979.

27. Interview, Dec. 6, 1980.

28. Interview, June 7, 1980

29. Wartburg Theological Seminary seminar, Feb. 28, 1979.

Chapter 5

1. See Xavier Rynne, *The Third Session* (New York: Farrar, Straus, and Giroux, 1965), p. 50.

2. *Pro Mundi Vita Boletín,* 62 (Sept./Oct. 1979) 3–4.

3. See Thomas C. Bruneau, "The Catholic Church and Development in Latin America," p. 537, and the LASA Session on Conflict of Loyalty, Bloomington, Ind., 1980.

4. Yves Congar, *Lay People in the Church* (Westminster, Md.: Newman, 1965) and *Priest and Laymen* (London: Chapman, 1966); Karl Rahner, "Notes on the Lay Apostolate," *Theological Investigations,* vol. 2 (Baltimore: Helicon, 1963), pp. 319–52, and *Christians in the Market Place* (New York: Sheed and Ward, 1966).

5. Interview with Sister Hermengarda Alves, deputy secretary, *Confederación Latinoamericana de Religiosos* (CLAR), March 10, 1981.

6. Opening Address at the Puebla Conference, John Eagleson and

Philip Scharper, eds., *Puebla and Beyond* (Maryknoll, N.Y.: Orbis, 1979), pp. 57–71.

7. See Clodovis Boff, *Comunidade eclesial, comunidade política* (Petrópolis: Vozes, 1978); P. Demo, *Comunidade: Igreja na Base* (São Paulo: Paulinas, 1974); and *SEDOC* (Petrópolis: Vozes), nos. 81, 95, 115, and 118.

8. See Alvin Lingran and Norman Shawchuck, *Let My People Go: Empowering the Laity* (Nashville: Abingdon, 1980).

9. See Gottfried Deelen, "La Iglesia al encuentro del pueblo en América Latina," *Pro Mundi Vita Boletín,* 81 (April/June 1980) 18–19, and Bishop Tiago Cloin, "The BCC Will Produce a New Kind of Priest," LADOC, *Basic Christian Communities*, pp. 41–44.

10. Press conference, Puebla, Feb. 8, 1979.

11. Studies on women in Latin America have multiplied rapidly in recent years. Some noteworthy collections of articles or books include: June D. Hahner, ed., *Women in Latin America: Their Lives and Views* (Los Angeles: University of California, Latin American Center, 1981, rev. ed.); Christine A. Loveland and Franklin O. Loveland, eds., *Sex Roles and Social Change in Native Lower Central American Societies* (Urbana: Illinois University of Press, 1981); June Nash and Helen Icken Safa, eds., *Sex Roles and Class in Latin America: Women's Perspectives on Politics, Economics, and the Family in the Third World* (Brooklyn: Bergin, 1980); Dinah Silveira de Queiroz, *Women of Brazil* (New York: Vintage, 1981); and Margaret Randall, *Women in Cuba: Twenty Years Later* (Brooklyn: Smyrna, 1981).

12. Interview, Cardinal Aloisio Lorscheider, Jan. 29, 1979.

Chapter 6

1. Press conference at CENCOS, Puebla, Feb. 1, 1979. See also Rafael Roncagliolo and Fernando Reyes Matta, *Iglesia, prensa, y militares* (Mexico City: Instituto Latinoamericano de Estudios Transnacionales, 1978).

2, "The Long Path to Puebla," in John Eagleson and Philip Scharper, eds., *Puebla and Beyond* (Maryknoll, N.Y.: Orbis, 1979).

3. The body of works on the role of the military in society has grown immensely since 1960. Many writings on the military in developed societies proved to have limited application to the contemporary situation in Latin America. However, several works on the military in the Third World that have appeared in the last ten years are especially helpful: Eric A. Nordlinger, *Soldiers and Politics: Military Coups and Governments* (Englewood Cliffs, N.J.: Prentice-Hall, 1977); Amos Perlmutter, *The*

Military and Politics in Modern Times: of Professionals, Pretorians, and Revolutionary Soldiers (New Haven: Yale University Press, 1977); Amos Perlmutter and Valerie Plave Bennett, eds., *The Political Influence of the Military: A Comparative Reader* (New Haven: Yale, 1980); Steffen W. Schmidt and Gerald A. Dorfman, eds. *Soldiers in Politics* (Los Altos, Cal.: Geron-X, 1974); Edward Feit, *The Armed Bureaucrats: Military-Administrative Regimes and Political Development* (Boston: Houghton-Mifflin, 1973); Kenneth Fidel, ed., *Militarism in Developing Countries* (New Brunswick, N.J.: Transaction Books, 1975); William R. Thompson, *The Grievances of Military Coup-Makers* (Beverly Hills, Cal.: Sage, 1973) and Gavin Kennedy, *The Military in the Third World* (New York: Scribner's, 1974). Excellent essays and full-length studies and dissertations on the Latin American military have built up a noteworthy corpus, lead by Alfred Stepan's pioneering work, *The Military in Politics: Changing Patterns in Brazil* (Princeton University Press, 1971). See also Brian Loveman and Thomas M. Davies, eds., *The Politics of Antipolitics: The Military in Latin America* (Lincoln: University of Nebraska Press, 1978); Abraham F. Lowenthal, ed., *Armies and Politics in Latin America* (New York: Holmes and Meier, 1976); Juan J. Linz and Alfred Stepan, eds., *The Breakdown of Democratic Regimes: Latin America* (Baltimore: Johns Hopkins University Press, 1978); Philippe C. Schmitter, ed., *Military Rule in Latin America: Functions, Consequences, and Perspectives* (Beverly Hills, Cal.: Sage, 1973); Philippe Faucher, *Le Brésil des militaires* (Montreal: l'Université de Montréal, 1981); Henry H. Keith and Robert A. Hayes, eds., *Perspectives on Armed Politics in Brazil* (Tempe: Center for Latin American Studies, Arizona State University, 1976); Frederick M. Nunn, *The Military Coup d'Etat as a Political Process: Ecuador, 1948–66* (Baltimore: Johns Hopkins, 1977); James O. Icenhour, "The Military in Colombian Politics," Ph.D. dissertation, George Washington University, 1976; Victor Villanueva, *Ejército Peruano: Del caudillismo anárquico al reformismo militar* (Lima: Mejía Baca, 1973); José Z. García, "Military Factions and Military Interventions in Latin America," in Sheldon Smith, ed., *The Military and Security in the Third World* (Boulder: Westview, 1978); Robert H. Miller, "Military Government and Approaches to National Development: A Comparative Analysis of the Peruvian and Panamanian Experiences," Ph.D. dissertation, University of Miami, 1975; Virgilio Rafael Beltrán, "The Army and Structural Changes in 20th-Century Argentina," in Jacques van Doorn, ed., *Armed Forces and Society: Sociological Essays* (The Hague: Mouton, 1968); Bruce R. Drury, "Civil-Military Relations and Military Rule: Brazil Since 1964," in George A. Kourvetaris and Betty A. Dobratz, eds., *World Perspectives in the Sociology of the Mili-*

tary (New Brunswick, N.J.: Transaction Books, 1977); and Luis A. Perez, Jr., *Army Politics in Cuba, 1898–1958* (University of Pittsburgh Press, 1976).

4. Violations are well documented by international groups such as Amnesty International and by national and diocesan commissions on human rights such as the Vicaría de Solidaridad (Santiago). Two very useful descriptions of human rights violations and the activities of human rights commissions are those by Penny Lernoux, *Cry of the People* (New York: Doubleday, 1980) and Brian H. Smith, "Churches and Human Rights in Latin America: Recent Trends on the Subcontinent," in Daniel H. Levine, ed., *Churches and Politics in Latin America* (Beverly Hills, Cal.: Sage, 1980), pp. 155–83. Extensive reporting of human rights violations since 1975 is provided by Human Rights International (1502 Ogden St., N.W., Washington, D.C. 20010).

5. See W. F. Barber and C. N. Ronning, eds., *Internal Security and Military Power: Counter-Insurgency and Civic Action in Latin America* (Colombus: Ohio State Unviersity Press, 1966), and M. Francis, "Military Aid to Latin America in the United States Congress," *Journal of Inter-American Studies*, 6 (July 1964) 389–401. *NACLA Report* has documented, since the mid-1960s, U.S. military assistance to Latin American countries. See also Lernoux, *Cry*, pp. 155–202.

6. Interview, Washington, D.C., March 26, 1970.

7. Statistics on the proportion of foreign clergy in the Latin American churches are nonexistent or have been collected in only a few countries. The single exception seems to be the 1965 calculations of the CELAM secretariat. Of the twenty-one national churches listed, twelve had more than 50 percent foreign clergy. See *Pro Mundi Vita*, 22 (1968) and *Pro Mundi Vita Special Note*, 15 (1970).

8. Sheila Cassidy, *Audacity to Believe* (Cleveland: Collins/World, 1978), and Pedro Casaldáliga, *I Believe in Justice and Hope* (Notre Dame, Ind.: Fides/Claretian, 1978). See also Teófilo Cabestrero, *Mystic of Liberation: A Portrait of Bishop Pedro Casaldáliga of Brazil* (Maryknoll, N.Y.: Orbis, 1981).

9. "Latin American Bishops Discuss Human Rights," LADOC Keyhole Series, nos. 15 and 16 (Washington: U.S. Catholic Conference, n.d.). See also "Repression against the Church in Brazil, 1968–78," LADOC Keyhole Series, no. 18; Paulo Evaristo Arns, *En defensa dos dereitos humanos: Encontro com o repore* (Rio de Janeiro: Civilazação Brasileira, 1978); Carlos Alberto Libânio Christo (Frei Betto), *Against Principalities and Powers* (Maryknoll, N.Y.: Orbis, 1976); Smith, "Churches and Human Rights," pp. 184–85.

10. For a summary statement and bibliography of the doctrine of na-

tional security and the reaction of the church to it, see "Las iglesias latinoamericanas frente al estado e ideología de la seguridad nacional," *Pro Mundi Vita Boletín*, no. 71 (March/April 1978). A shorter summary is found in "The Brazilian Church and Human Rights," *Pro Mundi Vita Dossiers* (Sept./Oct. 1977), pp. 5-16. José Comblin has written the most extensive response from the point of view of a philosopher-theologian in *The Church and the National Security State* (Maryknoll, N.Y.: Orbis, 1979). (Comblin, though, assumes military men have all internalized the doctrine and he tends to give an abstract doctrine a life of its own). CELAM issued the conclusions of an ad hoc study group that reported to the bishops: *La seguridad nacional: ¿Doctrina o ideología?* (Bogotá: CELAM, 1977). Relationships of national security doctrine and human rights are explored at length in "National Security Ideology and Human Rights," in Margaret E. Crahan, ed., *Human Rights and Basic Needs in the Americas* (Washington: Georgetown University Press, 1982).

11. Padín's name is variously spelled with an "n" or "m." The CELAM *Guía eclesiástica latinoamericana* (Bogotá: CELAM, 1980), p. 64, uses Padín. His working paper, "La doctrina de la seguridad nacional a la luz de la doctrina de la Iglesia," appears in Roberto Magni and Luis Zanotti, *America Latina: La Chiesa si contesta* (Rome: Editora Ruiniti, 1967), pp. 240-67.

12. Departamento de Acción Social, CELAM, meeting in Lima, April 30 to May 5, 1975. José Comblin prepared the background paper, "La doctrina de la seguridad nacional," published in *La Iglesia y la integración Andina* (Bogotá: CELAM, 1976), pp. 237-56.

13. Puebla General Conference, Final Document, §1247.

14. Puebla General Conference, Final Document, §§67, 480ff., 1260, and 1267. In the bishops' Preface, "Letter to the Peoples of Latin America," they stated: "Another thing that sends a shudder through our heart and marrow is the arms race, which continues to engender instruments of death. It involves the sad ambiguity of confusing the right of national defense with the ambitious pursuit of illicit profits. It will not serve to fashion peace."

15. See, however, A. Ferner, "A New Development Model for Peru: Anomalies and Readjustments," *Bulletin of the Society of Latin American Studies* (April 1978), pp. 42-62, and E. Dore and J. Weeks, "The Intensification of the Assault against the Working Class in 'Revolutionary' Peru," *Latin American Perspectives*, 3, 2 (Spring 1976) 55-83. See also Victor Villanueva, "Peru's 'New' Military Professionalism: The Failure of the Technocratic Approach," and Henry A. Dietz, "Mobilization, Austerity, and Voting: The Legacy of the Revolution for Lima's Poor," in Stephen M. Gorman, ed., *Post-Revolutionary Peru: The Poli-*

tics of Transformation (Boulder: Westview, 1982), pp. 157-78 and 73-99.

16. Loveman and Davies conclude: "In none of the five countries [Argentina, Bolivia, Brazil, Chile, and Peru] has military rule truly benefited the rural and working classes from the standpoint of improved income levels or availability of public services" (*The Politics*, pp. 226). See chapters by Thompson, Rock, Fishlow, Flynn, Saunders, Lowenthal, and Cotler in Loveman and Davies, *The Politics*, pp. 229-306. See also Evans, *Dependent Development,* passim; Alejandro Portes, "Housing Policy, Urban Poverty, and the State," *Latin American Research Review*, 14, 2 (1979) 3-24; Oscar Catalán and Jorge Arrate, "Chile: La política del régimen militar a las nuevas formas de desarrollo en América Latina," *Boletín de Estudios Latinoamericanos y del Caribe*, 25 (Dec. 1978) 51-72; and Elizabeth W. Dore and John F. Weeks, "Economic Performance and Basic Needs: The Examples of Brazil, Chile, Mexico, Nicaragua, Peru, and Venezuela," in Crahan, *Human Rights*, pp. 150-87. The bishops at the Puebla conference, not singling out military governments, spoke of the poor getting poorer (§§ 30 and 1264). One of the more recent criticisms of the way the Brazilian military government was handling the economy took place at the Brazilian Bishops' Conference annual meeting, April 6-15, 1983 (NC News Service dispatch no. 780, 1983).

17. Sylvia Ann Hewlett, *The Cruel Dilemmas of Development: Twentieth-Century Brazil* (New York: Basic Books, 1980), p. 166.

18. *The Politics*, p. 224.

19. *Armed Bureaucrats*, p. 11.

20. Medellín Conference, Document 7, § 20. Repeated by the Puebla Conference, Final Document, § 1247.

21. See esp. Brian H. Smith, *The Church and Politics in Chile: Challenges to Modern Catholicism* (Princeton University Press, 1982); Thomas C. Bruneau, *The Church in Brazil: The Politics of Religion* (Austin: University of Texas, 1982); and Daniel H. Levine, *Religion and Politics in Latin America: The Catholic Church in Venezuela and Colombia* (Princeton University Press, 1981).

22. Puebla Conference, Final Document, § 516.

23. Ibid., § 549.

24. James A. Malloy, "Bolivia: The Sad and Corrupt End of the Revolution," *USFI Reports South America,* no. 3, 1982, p. 1.

25. See esp. recent issues of *Clamor* (Comité de Defensa de los Derechos Humanos en el Cono Sur, Comisión Archdiocesana de la Pastoral de los Derechos Humanos y Marginados de São Paulo); *Brecha* (Centro de Información y Documentación Pedro Velázquez, Mexico City); and *Latinamerica Press* (Lima).

Conclusion

1. The influence of the Latin American church can be observed not only in the spread of liberation thought, basic Christian communities (often called small Christian communities or small churches in Asia or Africa), and dependency analysis, but also in the agendas and dynamics of international church meetings. See, especially, reports from and accounts of Synod meetings of selected bishops called to Rome to discuss larger issues facing the church. See also reports of Inter-American meetings of representatives of religious orders, especially meetings of the Leadership Conference of Women Religious with their Canadian and Latin American counterparts. The influence of the Latin Americans on a foreign episcopal conference is clearest in the case of Canada; see Christopher Lind, "Ethics, Economics, and Canada's Catholic Bishops," *Canadian Journal of Political and Social Theory,* 8, 3 (Fall 1983) 150-66.

2. See Richard Millet, *Guardians of the Dynasty* (Maryknoll, N.Y.: Orbis, 1978), and John A. Booth, *The End and the Beginning: The Nicaraguan Revolution* (Boulder: Westview, 1982).

3. See Booth, *The End*, pp. 134-37.

4. Ibid., pp. 143-44.

5. Details of the CELAM campaign are recounted in *Liaisons Internationales*, 24 (May 1981) 3-6.

6. Dirección Nacional del Frente Sandinista de Liberación Nacional, "Comunicado Oficial de la Dirección Nacional del F.S.L.N. sobre la Religión," *Barricada*, Oct. 7, 1980.

7. On Ernesto Cardenal, and two other priests in the Nicaraguan government, see Teófilo Cabestrero, *Ministers of God, Ministers of the People: Testimonies of Faith from Nicaragua* (Maryknoll, N.Y.: Orbis, 1983).

8. See *NACLA Report on the Americas*, 16, 1 (Jan.-Feb. 1982), 1-45.

9. See *Wall Street Journal* (Sept. 21, 1982), p. 1, and Thomas G. Sanders, "Brazil's Labor Unions" *USFI Reports South America,* no. 48 (1981), pp. 1-11.

10. See, for example, U.S. Catholic Conference, *Statement of the United States Catholic Conference on Central America*, Nov. 19, 1981 (Washington, D.C.) and "USCC Testimony on Central America," *Origins* 12, 41 (March 24, 1983), 649, 651-56. See also Thomas E. Quigley, "The Catholic Church and El Salvador," *Cross Currents*, 32, 2 (Summer 1982) 179-92, and "Where the Bishops Stand," *El Salvador Report*, 1, 7 (May/June 1981) 1, and Donald T. Libby, "Listen to the Bishops," *Foreign Policy* 52 (Fall 1983) 78-95.

Index